I0886324

3

EAGLES OF THE LUFTWAFFE

DFS 230 COMBAT GLIDER

NEIL PAGE

TEMPEST BOOKS

ACKNOWLEDGEMENTS

It is of course impossible to compile a book like this without leaning on the expertise of others, so it is very much a team effort. Firstly, I should like to thank Greg Way. Greg is the author of the recommended book Fallschirmjäger (Helion, 2020). Not only did he point me in the direction of his two-hour discussion on the DFS 230 on Paul Woodage's WW2TV and the Bundesarchiv RL 33 files, his knowledge enabled some of the more 'obscure' images to be properly captioned. Many of these photos have been rescued from long-lost albums by Paul Stipdonk, Michael Meyer and Del Davis and are published here for the first time. There would be no book without them. Nor could this brief history of the DFS 230 have been compiled without the generous contributions of Belgian author Jean-Louis Roba. Jean-Louis has written on Ében-Émael and Gran Sasso for Lela Presse and graciously allowed me to consult and 'exploit' his archive on Luftwaffe gliders and forwarded many photographs from his own extensive collection. Ian Tannahill, co-author of The Silent Attack – the most comprehensive English-language account of Ében-Émael – was another generous contributor. Finally, anybody writing on the DFS 230 owes a debt of gratitude to Georg Schlaug for his seminal work Die deutschen Lastensegler Verbände 1937-1945. It is unfortunately the case that the families of some of the men most closely associated with the DFS 230 refuse to talk to writers and researchers. Finally, sincere thanks to 'documentaliste' Nicolas Férard at the ECPA-D, who researched and captioned images by a PK Berichter who was KIA in Italy over 80 years ago, Wolfgang Stocker. Visiting the ECPA-D's 'German Collection' (le Fonds Allemand) in the Paris suburb of Ivry-sur-Seine should be on the 'bucket list' of every WWII 'enthusiast', reader, researcher and modeller.

First published in Great Britain in 2025
by Tempest Books
an imprint of Mortons Books Ltd.
Media Centre
Morton Way
Horncastle LN9 6JR

www.mortonsbooks.co.uk

ISBN 978-1-911704-26-3

Typeset by Jayne Clements (jayne@hinoki.co.uk), Hinoki Design and Typesetting

CONTENTS

INTRODUCTION

By 30 April 1945, the Allied armies had divided Germany into two, while Russian forces had fought their way into Berlin and stood just a few hundred metres away from the Reichs Chancellery and the Führer's bunker. At 0200 that morning a heavily-laden steel tubular-framed canvas and plywood skinned DFS 230 glider, its long slim wings and slender fuselage weighted down with Panzerfaust anti-tank weapons and munitions, struggled to get airborne behind a He 111 Schleppmaschine tug from the airfield of Hohenmauth near Königgrätz (today a town in the Czech Republic). Its destination was Breslau – a 'fortress' pocket far behind Soviet lines that the Russians had been besieging for months.

At the controls of the glider was an Uffz Thies, while the He 111 was being flown by Oblt Hörning, a Staffelkapitän in the Luftwaffe's last glider tow/transport unit, Schleppgruppe 1. At that stage of the war, good glider pilots were few and far between and the weight of the DFS 230 essentially committed it to a descending glide with little option to do anything else. The takeoff was without incident and the flight was initially trouble free.

Over the eastern slopes of the Riesengebirge mountain range, however, the Heinkel tug and DFS 230 encountered strong gusts of wind. Mid-air turbulence riding the air-pressure 'bow wave' behind the tug exerted huge forces on the cable – "...like water-skiing behind a speedboat..." Suddenly there was a whiplash of cable, as it slapped against the plexiglass canopy – in the turbulent air the tow cable had snapped.

Glider pilot Thies heard the roar of the Heinkel's engines fading into the night. Soon all he could hear was the whistling of the slipstream, his glider at an altitude of 3,000m. The pilot quickly calculated that he could still reach his destination. He could see the glow of the burning city far off in the distance. As he approached Breslau, he still had sufficient height to search out a landing spot on the main thoroughfare that ran through the city. Suddenly, through the pall of smoke that hung over the city, searchlights flicked on and their beams of light started to converge towards him. Anti-aircraft fire opened up a ferocious barrage.

Moments later the glider's canopy took a direct hit. The plexiglass exploded around his head. Although severely dazed, the stunned pilot still had control of the aircraft. Thies had lost a lot of height. He desperately sought out a clear area to put down on, a difficult endeavour because everything as far as he could see was on fire. Eventually he sighted the flat surface he was

A DFS 230 A (WNr. 352) with retrofitted armament. The MG 15 on the roof of the fuselage enabled the crew to lay down suppressive fire when approaching the landing zone. The 'fixed' MG 34 strapped to the cockpit side was normally deployed on landing, but the trigger could be operated by Bowden cable or through the 'hand hole' in the side of the aircraft — there was a zip fastening underneath the butt. Note the rudimentary sight in front of the windscreen and the muzzle flash guard. A Henschel Hs 126 tug is in the background.

looking for and levelled out for a landing approach. Braking chute deployed, he realised that he was coming down into a cemetery. Abruptly there was a terrible crashing and splintering sound as the plywood and canvas craft was torn apart. And then everything went silent. Thies was still alive and apparently unscathed. He released his straps and clambered down from his wrecked glider, all at once realising that the fuselage of the aircraft had wedged firm behind two huge tombstones. The wings had been torn off, but had absorbed the full force of the impact on landing. The clock on the instrument panel was stopped at 0305. Uffz Thies had survived what was probably the last flight of a DFS 230 during the Second World War.

The DFS 230 was (at first sight) a simple aircraft with its origins in the inter-war period when gliding was the only form of aviation permitted in Germany. Yet 'sponsored' by some of the leading lights of the new Luftwaffe and officially 'unveiled' in 1935, the DFS 230 was a critical piece of equipment ready to be deployed at a crucial phase of Hitler's so-called 'lightning war' on the West.

Contrary to the 'myth' of a powerful all-conquering force, the Luftwaffe, a relatively new air arm with many units still under-strength, had to improvise and innovate to make up for its lack of resources. Alongside the pairing of stuka and panzer, the combination of glider and paratrooper became a key element in the success of Blitzkrieg – the DFS 230 enabled the stealthy landing of sections of ten highly trained troops, "... riding like Valkyries into the vitals of a strategic objective".

The German 'coup de main' atÉben-Émael in May 1940 shocked the West. The speed and violence of this unprecedented airborne attack was repeated on Crete, a heavily defended island 'fortress', assaulted and captured from the air. But, by the turn of the year 1941-42, Blitzkrieg was no more. The DFS 230 was then operated primarily – at least on the Eastern Front – as a 'Lastensegler' (LS), a cargo glider, a complement to powered transport aircraft, able to carry one ton of fuel, food and munitions and put down in a very small area. Two DFS 230s had a similar transport capacity to one Junkers Ju 52. The latter were in short supply, especially after Crete and Stalingrad where hundreds of the vulnerable trimotor transports were lost. The DFS 230 was even sent to Stalingrad (well over 100 aircraft), although the likelihood of them being seriously deployed was minimal. Most failed to even arrive in southern Russia before 6. Armee capitulated.

The DFS 230 was one of very few Luftwaffe aircraft types still flying in the final days of the war. Munitions and food were being flown in to the defenders of Breslau and the inferno of Hitler's encircled capital city even as the Nazi dictator was preparing to take poison on 30 April 1945.

Following release of the tow rope or 'Ausklinken', this DFS 230 flies on to its destination. For the glider pilot, voice communication or 'Verständigung' with the 'Schleppmaschine' tug to confirm or determine the release point — for example — was possible via a cable along the tow rope through his 'Kehlkopfmicrofon' throat mike.
VIA PAUL STIPDONK

DFS 230 glider pilots in training, probably in Langendiebach during 1941.

1

GLIDING AND THE ORIGINS OF THE DFS 230

THE IDEA that as soon as he came to power in 1933 Adolf Hitler somehow set about creating a military aviation arm from scratch is one of those myths that have grown up around the Second World War Luftwaffe. The fact is, the pre-war Luftwaffe lacked aircraft, pilots and resources. The victors of the First World War had imposed harsh peace treaty terms aimed at permanently subduing the defeated Germans – reparations ostensibly payable until 1988 (!), restricting the Germans to an army of 100,000 men and banning all military aviation. Gliding was unrestricted however. As a result, gliding clubs developed throughout Germany and enjoyed great popularity.

Gliding enabled the instruction of basic aeronautical principles and flying a sailplane required the sort of flight training that any prospective future military aviator would recognize. Leading Hungarian-American aerospace engineer Theodore von Kármán, who left Germany, before the arrival in power of the Nazis later said: "The Allies were short-sighted when they banned motorised flying in Germany. They stimulated the very development they wanted to stop, the growth of German aviation. Experiments with sport gliders sharpened German thinking in aerodynamics, structural design and meteorology."

The sport of gliding experienced an exceptional boom in the last years of the Weimar Republic and the Rhön Valley in Hesse became the 'Mecca' of gliding in Germany. Students from Darmstadt had flown the first gliders at the Wasserkuppe, the highest peak in the Rhön mountain range, as early as 1910. In 1922, Arthur Martens, a passionate glider pilot and later glider designer, founded the first glider school here. Martens himself was the first pilot to undertake a glider flight of more than one hour and his glider school proved very successful. For aspiring glider pilots who could not travel to the Wasserkuppe, there were several schools scattered throughout the country. But the calamitous economic situation in Germany during the period from 1919 to 1933 slowed down the development of the discipline. It was not until the National Socialists came to power that gliding developed irreversibly.

The creation of the NSFK (Nationalsozialistiches Fliegerkorps) in January 1932, one year before Adolf Hitler's election was key. A number of 'Alte Kameraden' and First World War aviators, Hermann Göring, Rudolf Hess and the great [illegible]

Ernst Udet, were not only close to the future Führer but determined to resurrect German aviation, both civilian and military branches. In 1933 the DLV (Deutsche Luftsport Verband) was created and this organisation seems to have been mainly reserved for party members (including those of the SA and SS formations).

In 1937 the NSFK assumed control of all equipment, effectively the umbrella organisation for all flying schools. This now paramilitary organisation had a hybrid status, as did its leader, the renowned Friedrich Christiansen, who had been a naval aviator in Flanders as early as 1915. Christiansen and many of his subordinates (like another Great War ace, Harry von Bülow-Bothkamp) had links with the Luftwaffe either as soldiers or reservists.

INTO SERVICE WITH THE LUFTWAFFE

Three years before Adolf Hitler became the new leader of Germany, in 1930, the Röhn-Rossitten-Gesellschaft (established close to the Wasserkuppe) under the leadership of engineer Alexander Lippisch completed the design of a new wide-span sailplane. Released into updrafts, with its 30m wingspan it could fly at very high altitudes and with its low sink-rate could be launched to "make meteorological observations" – or fly over enemy lines, observe and then return home. The project, designated 'Obs', was taken up and developed by the Deutsches Forschungsanstalt für Segelflug or DFS (German Glider Research Institute). The DFS had been established in 1933 by the nationalisation of the Rhön-Rossitten Gesellschaft (RRG) at Darmstadt to centralise all gliding activity in Germany, under the directorship of Professor Walter Georgii. Georgii was an academic meteorologist who had undertaken some of the first research into thermals for gliding flight and during the First World War had been a member of the Englandgeschwader, flying Gotha bombers over London.

The 'Obs' concept had already attracted the attention of Udet and aviatrix Hanna Reitsch had tested the prototype. Ingenieur Hans Jacobs – a prodigy of Lippisch's who had started his career as a shipbuilding apprentice in Hamburg – recalled how the 'Obs' concept evolved into the DFS 230: "The 'Obs' did not seem to us to be a project worth pursuing. Such an aircraft could be easily shot down during a daylight sortie and night-time recce missions were out of the question as the requisite infrared equipment did not exist at that time. However, we did believe that it would be possible to send a sailplane over enemy lines at dawn carrying 'saboteurs'. The aircraft could be towed to an altitude of 3,000-4,000m, released over friendly territory and come in over enemy lines silently to land at a specific target.

"I designed the DFS 230 to carry nine men and a pilot. The fuselage had to have as small a cross-section as possible. To work out the size of the fuselage we took a bench from the staff canteen and sat nine men astride it. We then moved two drawing boards to position them vertically on both sides and thus determined the minimum necessary width of the fuselage. The idea was summarised in a memorandum with a detailed outline drawing and forwarded to Udet. He decided that we should build a mock-up as quickly as possible."

Udet assessed the possibilities of the machine and brought it to the attention of other Imperial Air Force veterans, men such as Robert Ritter von Greim, and those involved in the re-establishment of German aviation such as Kesselring, who were close to Göring – 'visionaries' according to some, who could perhaps see the potential of a 'combat' glider. The mock-up was presented to Udet and his staff in September 1936; Udet had by then been appointed head of the Technical Office in the Reichsluftfahrtministerium – the German Air Ministry. The exact date of the first flight is not known but by January 1937, the first prototype had been completed and tested. The DFS 230 V2 and V3 prototypes were completed shortly afterwards. Udet travelled from Berlin to Darmstadt, headquarters of the DFS, in person to watch flight testing in progress. According to Jacobs, Udet pronounced himself satisfied and set a date by which the first Luftwaffe pilots for the DFS 230 were to be trained.

A modification of the original 'Obs' design, the DFS 230 was a braced shoulder-wing glider with a wingspan of 21.98m and a very small cross-section. The box-shaped fuselage was constructed from a lattice-work of steel tubes covered with canvas and plywood and was 11.24m long. According to Kershaw, "...care had to be taken on entry and leaving so as not to accidentally poke holes with weapons through the thin outer skin." The nose of the glider was solidly reinforced to enable it to land on very rough ground. The two-wheeled take-off dolly was jettisoned shortly after leaving the ground, while landings were carried out on a ski-like skid attached to the middle of the fuselage underside.

On 11 January 1937, two experienced parachutists, Lt Walter Kiess and Uffz Flucke, arrived in Darmstadt, to familiarise themselves with the new machine. Over the following months the two Fallschirmjäger also trained as instructors and on 1 April 1937, a training programme for glider pilots began at the Darmstadt-Griesheim aerodrome with around 60 students. A second session took place from November 1937 to June 1938 under the aegis of the 'Lastensegler Kommando Kiess'. This included a combined glider/paratrooper exercise on 16 November, during which the clear superiority of the glider loaded with soldiers (Luftlandetruppen) was demonstrated for the first time. Paratroops jumping from a Ju 52 took 15 minutes to capture the designated target, while infantrymen dropped off nearby via DFS 230 gliders took just three.

These experiments could have been short-lived, however, as on 19 July 1938 the newly formed LS-Ausbildungskommando ('training detachment' attached to the Ju 52 KG z.b.V 1) was disbanded, its personnel returned to their original units, and the DFS 230s handed over to the Luftwaffesportverein (Luftwaffe sports association). This may have been the result of a lack of funds. In other words the Luftwaffe – which had undergone rapid expansion partly as a result of the training dispensed by various Segelflieger units (DLV, NSFK and HJ) – was to be deprived of its only glider unit. As luck would have it however, Generalmajor Kurt Student, who had recently been placed in charge of German airborne forces (and had flown gliders as early as 1921), was confronted during the Sudeten Crisis (September 1938) with a chronic shortage of transport capacity. There were insufficient aircraft to ensure the transfer of his Fallschirmjäger to Czechoslovakia. Looking for alternatives, Student heard about Kommando Kiess and contacted its commander. Shortly afterwards, Student's 7. Fliegerdivision was assigned a LS-Kommando (glider detachment) with six Ju 52s, six DFS 230s, two officers and 27 NCOs and soldiers. The attack on Czechoslovakia did not materialise, but the Kommando survived and the 'Lastensegler' concept grew in importance.

In January 1939, the LS-Kdo Flg. Div. 7 moved to Burg/Magdeburg to expand, gradually receiving resources and personnel. A year later, in January 1940 (three months after the outbreak of the Second World War), the Luftwaffe Segelflugschule (glider school) was established in Braunschweig-Waggum, later known as the Fl.Schule der Lw (S) 1 or Ergänzungsgruppe (S) 1. Initially led by Hptm Arnold Willerding (from a Ju 52 unit), the glider school was assigned eight Ju 52s from 17./KG z.b.V. 5, in addition to twenty DFS 230s. This school was to speed up the training of glider pilot candidates.

First World War fighter ace, inter-war stunt pilot and associate of Göring, Ernst Udet (shown here in 1935) was an excellent glider pilot and played a key role in pushing forward the DFS 230 project.

Glider commander Hptm Walter Kiess, seen here following his award of the Ritterkreuz on 12 May 1940. VIA IAN TANNAHILL

Nationalsozialistisches
Fliegerkorps NSFK
Förderer-Ausweis Nr. 32323
für
Hempel Hans
(Zuname, Vorname oder Firma)
Nordhausen, Fliegerhorst 3. Staffel
(Wohnort, Straße, Hausnummer)
Bordmechaniker, Syrau/Vogtl. 27.3.1
(Beruf, Geburtsort und -Datum)
Nordhausen, den
Ort, Datum
Stempel und Unterschrift der NSFK-Aufnahmestelle
Der Korpsführer
Generalmajor
Eigenhändige Unterschrift des Inhabers:

NSFK identity card belonging to Hans Hempel. Hempel was previously an aircraft mechanic with KG 4 before applying to fly gliders in the Luftwaffe. The NS-Fliegerkorps was intended as a 'preparatory school' for the Luftwaffe ('Segelfliegen im NS-Fliegerkorps, der Weg zur Luftwaffe'), but, more sinisterly, mixed glider pilot instruction with potent Nazi ideology and propaganda. Hempel flew a DFS 230 into action at Ében-Émael with Gruppe 'Beton'. VIA IAN TANNAHILL

During the Sudeten crisis, Generalmajor Kurt Student included a DFS 230 unit in his 7. Fliegerdivision. Like a number of the Luftwaffe hierarchy, he was a First World War fighter ace. As the driving force behind German airborne forces (Fallschirmjäger and Luftlandetruppen), he quickly came to the attention of Hitler who, to quote Kershaw, "regarded airborne troops as one of his secret weapons". Student is seen here wearing the Ritterkreuz he was awarded on 12 May 1940.

Hanna Reitsch made some of the first flights of the DFS 230. Seen here in a DFS Stummel Habicht, Reitsch flew in the German glider team at the 1936 Berlin Olympics.

'D-5-289' was the DFS 230 V1. Note the rounded nose and a single-piece canopy. On 19 October 1940 this aircraft successfully landed (and took off again via a so-called 'bungee' launch) on one of Austria's highest summits, the Großvenediger .

Two more views of D 5-289. VIA PAUL STIPDONK

A rare view of the second DFS 230 constructed. Note the absence of the window 'portholes' in the fuselage. VIA PAUL STIPDONK

An early DFS 230 with the rounded nose and single-piece canopy. Note the fuselage aft of the cockpit was 'solid'. 'Folding' hatches behind the cockpit to facilitate entry and exit were introduced from the A-2 variant.

The DFS 230 was towed aloft on a wheeled dolly — built by Arado — that was jettisoned once airborne at heights of between 5-15m. The spring-braced central landing skid was made of ash — a hard wood — and metal skinned. VIA PAUL STIPDONK

A DFS 230 during the winter of 1939-1940.

2

BLITZKRIEG IN THE WEST! ÉBEN-ÉMAEL AND THE ALBERT CANAL BRIDGES

THE WEHRMACHT launched Fall Gelb ('Case Yellow'), Hitler's 'great' offensive in the West, on 10 May 1940. It was an offensive that went far beyond the erroneous name of 'Battle of France' and comprised several key thrusts. Firstly, paratroops and ground troops were tasked with violating Dutch neutrality, drawing the French northwards. At the same time, the Panzer divisions were to push towards the heart of Belgium (which was also neutral) to hold down the Belgian army and the Franco-British units that would inevitably advance into the country. While the Allies were preoccupied with these two combined attacks, armoured units were tasked with crossing what the French thought were the 'impassable' Ardennes to carry out the famous 'coup de faux' (Sichelschnitt), the encirclement of Allied troops too far north.

Although the attack on the Netherlands and the advance into the Ardennes were risky, in principle these manoeuvres were unlikely to come up against serious obstacles during their first few days. This was not the case for the central thrust of the operation however: the penetration of Belgium. In August 1914 the German advance into France had been held up by Belgian fortifications. In 1940 any delay to the German advance would have jeopardised Fall Gelb; German tanks had to penetrate as deep as possible into Belgium, concentrate Allied attention there and facilitate the breakthrough into the Ardennes. Since 1914, however, things had changed considerably on the German-Belgian border.

In the early 1930s, the Belgian government had a canal dug to link the (then) prosperous metallurgical basin of Liège to the (still) major port of Antwerp. This canal (called the 'Albert canal' in honour of the Belgian sovereign of the Great War) ran more or less north-south, linking the Meuse to the Scheldt and indirectly forming a real anti-tank barrier. Part of this was the canyon-like Caster trench. To further complicate the task of the Fall Gelb planners, an imposing fortress had been built above the Caster trench as early as 1931: Ében-Émael. The fort was a huge structure of some 66 hectares – 40 of which constituted the surface area of the central massif – a kilometre

Assembly of the gliders prior to Ében-Émael. Note the absence of national markings. VIA IAN TANNAHILL

Interior view of a DFS 230. This must have been the very spartan layout of the first models, as tubular seats were later installed in the fuselage.

long and 700m wide (the 'blind' wall of the Caster trench forming its north-eastern flank). It bristled with guns of all calibres, capable of taking on an adversary whatever the direction of attack. In 1938, the Belgian author and journalist Charles d'Ydewalle wrote emphatically: "Just as the feudal baron barricaded himself in his castle, Belgium has its own barricade with a moat, and that moat is the Albert Canal. Ében-Émael's castle is buried in the ground, with its network of corridors, its flanking structures and its view of Saint-Pierre mountain. It looks like a colossal termite mound…"

The task facing German strategists was therefore a complex one. Not only did they have to capture this formidable structure, but they also had to take intact the three nearby bridges (Canne, Vroenhoven and Veldwezelt) spanning the canal, which were essential for the passage of vehicles. Everything had to happen at the same time, because disabling the fortress if the bridges had been blown put an end to any hope of a rapid advance. And neutralising the Belgian garrisons guarding the bridges was pointless as long as the fortress could hold the whole sector under fire from its powerful guns...

According to certain sources, it was Hitler himself who insisted on the deployment of squads of paratroopers landing silently behind enemy lines, transported by DFS 230 gliders. Delivering a rapid and fatal thrust was the 'essence' of Blitzkrieg. The decision though stunned the OKW – a handful of men were to be entrusted with the fate of the complex campaign in the West! In the event of failure, the German army would once again stall in front of Liège, losing men, while the two wings of the offensive (the Netherlands and the Ardennes) would see their advance slowed if not halted.

On 3 November 1939, the men of 7. Fliegerdivision (parachute division) received secret instructions. On the first day of the offensive in the West, the bridges of Veldwezelt, Vroenhoven and Canne as well as the fort of Ében-Émael were to be seized in a 'coup de main' – with the help of the Koch assault group. The 4. Pz Div arriving shortly afterwards would cross the canal and enlarge the bridgeheads. The 151. IR would take care of the final annihilation of Ében-Émael, while further north, special units would seize bridges near Maastricht.

The first company of Hptm Walther Koch's 1. FJR, an engineer section led by Oblt Rudolf Witzig as well as a detachment of gliders under the orders of Hptm Walter Kiess subsequently assembled at Hildesheim airfield where they would form the Sturmabteilung Koch (assault group Koch).

As Luftwaffe glider specialist Georg Schlauch explained: "An LS-Versuchsflug of 30 men and 15 aircraft were deployed to Hildesheim. Designated 17./KG z.b.V. 5, it was reinforced by ten highly qualified glider pilots from the DFS and sports teams, augmented by 50 of Germany's best glider pilots ordered to report to Hildesheim by registered letter. Subsequently, further DFS 230s arrived from Anklam and Eschwege, bringing the unit strength at the beginning of December 1939 to 34 Junkers Ju 52s and 43 DFS 230s."

With training in full swing, paratroopers and pilots studied models of the fortress. While the paratroopers and sappers practised intensively (occasionally on Czech bunkers with concrete similar to that of the Belgian works), the pilots practised their landings. According to one of them: "We were called up one day for a briefing. Our leader told us that, from then on, we would be involved in an operation that went far beyond a normal secret mission. We were shown various photos. The first showed a deep chasm with steep, high walls. We were told that beyond the one on the right a fortification had been built into the mountain.

"Other photos showed bridges over a canal and we were told that the river bank was heavily fortified with a bunker, infantry positions, anti-tank type 'dragon's teeth' obstacles and machine gun nests. Our landing areas would be on the roof of the fortification and near the fortified bridge positions. Regardless of the resistance, which would be very strong (we were talking about an entire division), it was imperative that we landed at the exact designated location. Back in our rooms, we discussed all this at length. For many, this mission was suicidal."

According to Belgian author J-L Lhoest, in March 1940 at Dedelstorf, Koch's assault sections completed preparations for the attack with the use of live ammunition and bombs, as well as wide scale Luftwaffe participation. The next stage of the operation was the transfer to Cologne's two Einsatzhafen (operational airfields): Ostheim and Butzweilerhof. To effect this transfer, the gliders were dismantled and transported in large, anonymous furniture vans in the greatest secrecy.

According to an organisation chart, the DFS 230 gliders were divided up according to the objectives:

* **Ében-Émael (Gruppe Granit):** eleven gliders.
* **Vroenhoven (Gruppe Beton):** nine gliders reinforced by two from the Stab.
* **Canne (Gruppe Eisen):** ten gliders.
* **Veldwezelt (Gruppe Stahl):** ten gliders.

In other words, the planned assault force comprised a total of 42 DFS 230s, each carrying an average of eight men. This was a small number for a simultaneous attack on four vital targets. J-L Lhoest noted that this was because "...quite simply the airfields around Cologne did not allow more than 42 tugs and a similar number of gliders to take off more or less at the same time." This explanation is open to question. One source reports that only 45 DFS 230s had been built by 1939. Although the production numbers for 1937 and 1938 are not known, this figure was certainly low thanks to the relative lack of interest in this machine on the part of the Luftwaffe hierarchy. And, in the early months of 1940, priority was almost certainly given to 'real' combat aircraft in

Gruppe Granit pilot Otto Bräutigam was an 'ace' pre-war glider pilot and instructor with several world records to his name, including a 502km flight from the Wasserkuppe in 1935. He also flew alongside Reitsch in the 1936 Berlin Olympics. Of note was his 'breathtaking' aerobatics as a pilot in the NSFK 'Kunstflug Kette' at the 'Reichsparteitag' in 1938. Ostensibly a civilian, he was one of a number of glider pilots 'co-opted' at short notice into the Ében-Émael assault force. He was killed in the crash of a Messerschmitt Me 321 transport glider in May 1941. LUFTWAFFEN REVUE

an air force undergoing major expansion. It can therefore be assumed that a maximum of only 80 DFS 230s were assembled at the Gotha factory between 1937 and April 1940, some of which were destroyed or damaged during exercises or training flights. The 42 DFS 230s earmarked for the Belgian operation probably therefore represented the entire German glider force capable of transporting 'parachutists' or 'Fallschirmer'. In addition, there were at least four gliders in reserve as replacement cover for the 42 'operational' gliders.

Some of the best pilots in the Third Reich were assigned to the special unit at Hildesheim. They included such 'names' in the world of gliding as Rudi Opitz, Otto Bräutigam and Erwin Ziller. These three were assigned to Ében-Émael along with nine other comrades. It took considerable skill to fly a glider loaded with a ton of ballast and land it precisely in a very small space – and the number of pilots who could do it was correspondingly small. This manoeuvre was vital for the attackers as they needed to get to within 20m of their target, bypassing the fortress's long-range weaponry and entering the zone of hand-to-hand combat from the very first seconds of engagement.

By March 1940, glider pilots were perfectly capable of taking off at night, in total darkness, flying in formation and landing in unfamiliar areas. Contrary perhaps to what is sometimes asserted, these ostensibly 'civilian' glider pilots had not received any infantry combat training. As for the pilots of the Ju 52 tugs, they were used to towing aircraft, day and night, alone or in formation and in Staffel strength, at the end of a 70m-long cable.

The glider pilots were the key to the success of the planned assault. According to Fallschirmjäger Wilhelm Alefs of Sturmgruppe Granit: "In theory, we were to attack the combat post at the northern end of the Ében-Émael fortress ... We were to land directly in front of the gun emplacements of two small armoured positions with the armoured cupola at our back. Studying the aerial photos, we deduced that the landing would be difficult, as trees on the north-east side prevented us from arriving by air. On the other side, the terrain was sloping. We decided not to come in from the west as we risked falling into the canal. A small undulation in the terrain could stop the machine and send it between the walls of the gap. So our pilot and I decided to come in from the east, turn south and follow the canal from the south to the northern tip. By banking to the left wing, we were going to reduce our speed. This would allow us to land our bird in the very small area available to us. All this with a glider loaded to the limit!"

A parachutist from the Gruppe Beton remembered: "I was in Hptm Koch's glider. He preferred to take smaller men with him, which meant he could load more equipment and ammunition into the gliders. On their own, Granit were taking in a long list of equipment ... six machine guns (with 13,000 rounds), 54 rifles (with 6,000 rounds), 83 pistols (with 5,000 rounds), 2,400kg of explosives, four flamethrowers, one radio, four flare pistols, 53 satchels of hand grenades, a smoke pot, various grenades, a 6m and six 4m ladders, two large bed sheets, 13 swastika flags, 83 torches, signs, sapper's tools etc."

The flags, signs and sheets were intended to make it easier to be spotted from the air, but also to send messages to Luftwaffe aircrews; the airborne troops would be supported by Ju 87 Stukas (from Stukageschwader 2) during their attack, while the ladders would be used to climb over walls and other obstacles and then climb the fort's cupolas.

THE ATTACK

In the hangar at Ostheim, paratroopers and pilots from Gruppe Granit received confirmation that the operation had been launched. There was immediate excitement. Uffz Karl-Heinz Lange remembered: "We were assigned to our aircraft, which were there ready for take-off. Each pilot supervised the loading of the equipment belonging to his parachute group, weapons, ammunition and explosives. Each pilot had to ensure that his

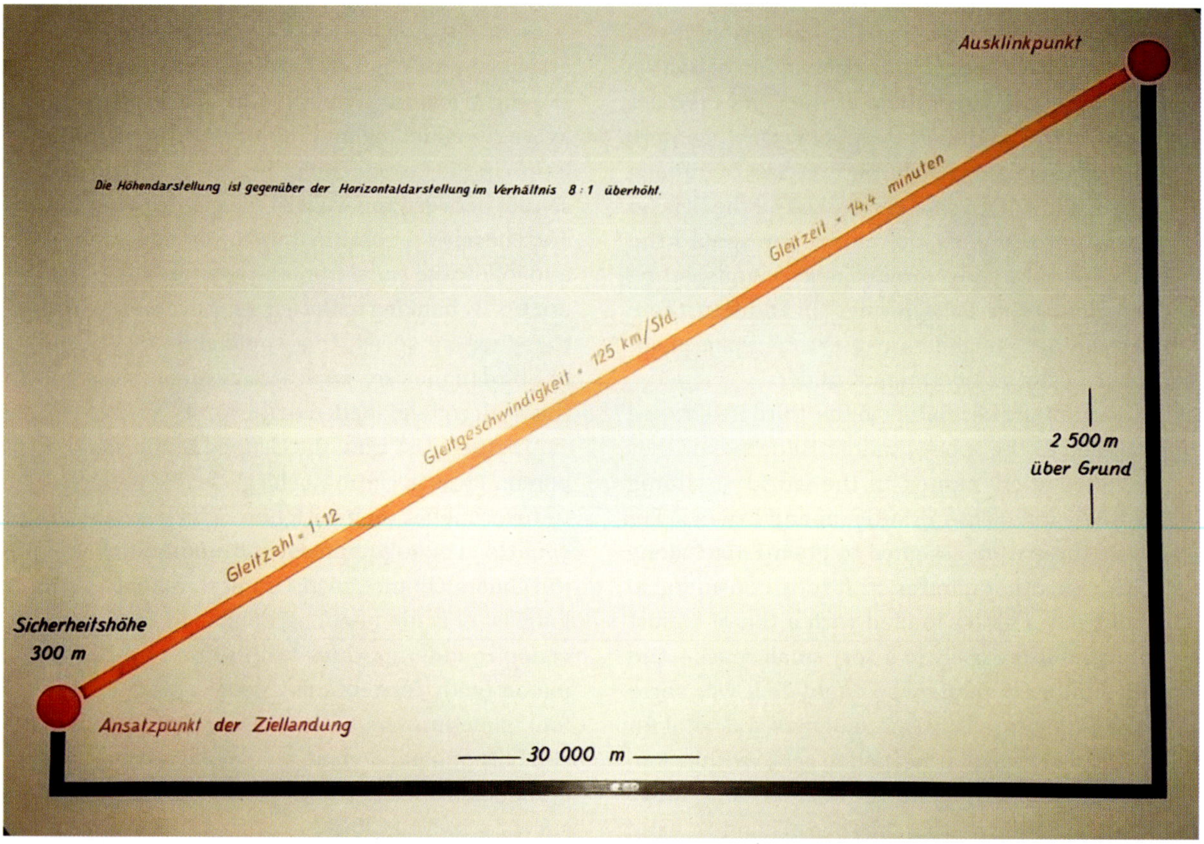

A graph showing the calculation for the glide onto the fort. The DFS 230 would separate from the tug ('Ausklinkpunkt') at an altitude of 2,500m and 30km from the objective (i.e. above Aachen). At a glide speed of 125km/h it would take the DFS 230 around 14 minutes to arrive over the target at a height of 300m to set up an approach for landing ('Ansatzpunkt der Ziellandung'). The DFS 230 was designed to be capable of a long approach, enabling it to be released a considerable distance from the target so the sound of the towing aircraft did not alert the enemy.

aircraft was airworthy, despite the weight. After loading, we were assembled and given the final operational orders confirming the precise objectives we had already worked on in Hildesheim using models. This gave us the certainty that our objective was indeed in Belgium."

Uffz Wilhelm Alefs of the Witzig pioneer group described the evening of 9 May 1940 and the departure: "At around 2000 the alarm was sounded ... Ju 52s landed. They taxied to the designated location. A board with a number was placed behind each aircraft. Each of our gliders also had one so that we wouldn't get the wrong aircraft in the night. We had nothing to do. We were in combat gear and our weapons were in the gliders. At 2105 the hangar doors were opened and the gliders were taken out. The tow cables were checked, as was the undercarriage. Discussions were held with the Ju 52 pilots. At 2130 each group returned to its glider.

"Everyone had to know exactly where his machine was ... We waited. Some played cards, others took a little nap. Everyone wrote a will ... We had been given Pervitin tablets to keep

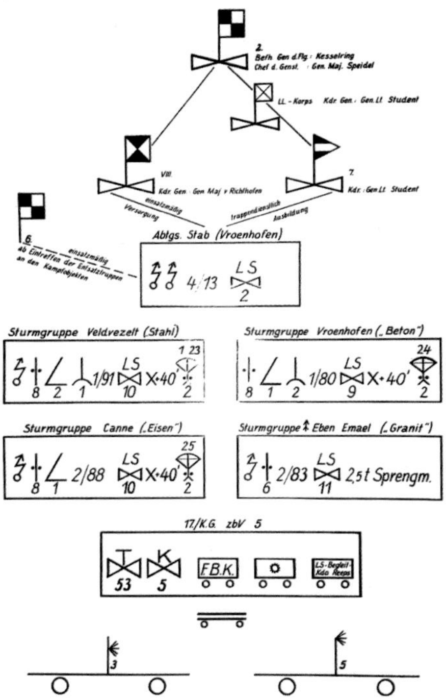

Organisation chart of the Sturmabteilung Koch with the distribution of gliders (LS = Lastensegler).

us awake. A glider pilot who swallowed three of them with a good sip of strong coffee didn't sleep for several days! ... Then came the order: 'Get in the gliders!' The boards with the machine numbers were lit by blacked-out paraffin lamps. We followed the order as we had said so many times before. The pilot entered through the rear door. I searched blindly under my seat. The explosives were there. My weapon was a rifle. Our Ju was warming up her engines and the blast of warm air literally shook us. Suddenly, we started moving. Our glider left the ground at Ostheim. We were flying into battle..."

This account is corroborated by the final report of Fw Gerhard Raschke, head of the Granit group. He specified that the load of each glider had been pushed to its maximum (1,200kg!) and that the skids of the DFS had been wrapped in a thick roll of barbed wire to increase the braking effect on landing.

The road to the west was lined with searchlights. They would stay on for 30 seconds, go off for another ten and then come back on. Lanterns scattered between Cologne and the border formed a 'road of light'.

Alefs continued: "We could feel the machine 'leaning' into the wind. Our tug was gaining altitude, engines at full throttle. Suddenly, the marker lights came on and our climb continued over this 'road of light'. At one point, our pilot had difficulty controlling the glider. The continuous loud engine noise prevented us from questioning him. Shortly afterwards, we learned that we had come across the Koch gliders that had left Butzweilerhof and had been caught in the turbulence..."

It must have been at this point that the young Obergefreiter Karl Pilz, piloting the glider carrying Lt Rudolf Witzig, was surprised by the sudden arrival of a Ju 52, forcing him to turn sharply. Under the strain, the tow cable snapped. Pilz landed the unintentionally released glider with ease. Witzig was appalled. His men were flying into battle and he would not be leading them... He went to great lengths to obtain a new Ju 52 and was able to resume his flight some three hours later. When Karl Pilz dropped him off with his group on the fort, his soldiers had already completed their mission.

Lt Witzig was not the only one to land prematurely. Near Düren, Uffz Fritz Bredenbeck saw his tug waggling its wings, a sign that the cable had to be released. This signal seemed highly dubious to him, given the reduced flight time, but as the Ju 52 pilot insisted, Bredenbeck complied. It was, however, an error on the part of the pilot of the towing aircraft who had confused the signals on the ground. Here, too, the pilot landed his glider without difficulty but, being too far from an airfield, the nine parachutists were unable to leave by air. They joined the ground troops moving towards Ében-Émael and fought on the ground.

Meanwhile, the airborne troops continued their flight. Uffz Alefs' account continues: "Our Ju 52 was climbing higher and higher. We must have been at 3,000m. It was getting light. Suddenly we felt a jerk. Our glider had been released and slowly the thunderous roar of the Ju 52's engines faded away. Position lights were extinguished. All we could hear was the sound of the wind: a steady rustle and the whistle of the wings. Now we could talk. The pilot was the first to break the silence: 'We are flying over the border. There's the Meuse. This is the Albert Canal'.

"We knew that we were only a few seconds away from the target. We could not see anything but we were caught in the fire of the anti-aircraft defences. It seems that this glider and a few others were not dropped at 3,000m but slightly lower, over an area of Dutch territory. Hence the Dutch flak: I tried to look out of the small window on my side. Bright coloured shells were bursting very close to us. Our group leader, leaning over the pilot's shoulder, shouted: 'There's the fort!' We in the cabin could not see anything. The flak was beginning to bother us. The shells were bursting closer and closer to our fragile glider. 'We are turning south', shouted the pilot, 'See the dome of the northern tip'. This change of direction allowed me to take a look and see our 'model' clearly. The pilot swooped down to land between the cupola and the two forts. The whistling of the slipstream grew louder.

"We were surrounded by gliders flying in all directions. It sounded like total confusion, but each aircraft was heading straight for its target. The earth rushed up to meet us. The pilot shouted out what was happening: 'We are coming in on the left'. Suddenly the glider banked over onto the left wing. We approached the ground and for a moment our aircraft seemed to be suspended in mid-air. But then we picked up speed again and the machine started to move forward again. Achtung! Landing! Exactly as planned. We clung to our seats. There was a sudden crack and then some splintering. One of us began to groan. "We were thrown on top of each other. My foot was caught under our load and the ladder we were carrying fell on me. 'Out! Get out!' shouted a comrade. But we were stuck fast. We pushed with all our might on the door, which finally gave way..."

Schüller already had two shaped charges in his hand and was running towards the cupola. Passmann tore off the flame thrower attached to the rear door and ran towards a door.

But it was the glider from Section 8 that landed first, despite anti-aircraft machine-gun fire. The pilot, Uffz Heinrich Diestelmeier, described the episode: "On 10 May 1940, I arrived from the east but was still too high for my calculations. I reached the top of the fort at 300m and there was still no other aircraft in sight. As I was still too high, I put my foot down to describe wide circles and lost height at a speed of 7m/s. My glider was hit by ground fire on the way down to the fort, but I managed to pitch it on the approach so that it wouldn't be too easy a target. This tactic worked very well. The glider took no more hits and remained intact; no one was hurt. I landed at 0524, just before dawn..."

Thus, even in the absence of Rudolf Witzig, the pioneers were able to carry out their assigned tasks effectively. The glider pilots had not yet been trained as infantrymen and most likely remained 'wisely' close to their aircraft, sometimes behind machine guns to cover their comrades who were scrambling from cupola to cupola, from armoured shelters to fortified positions.

As well as gliders, the Fallschirmjäger brought another 'novelty' to this modern war: shaped charges, unknown at the time to the other belligerents. These revolutionary explosives pulverised armour, sometimes shredding unfortunate servicemen who logically thought they were safe behind the steel shield of their cupolas. The force of the blasts rocked the superstructure of the fort, along with the smoke, dust and howls of the attackers, enough to destabilise a garrison of around a thousand men who were completely overwhelmed.

The explosions destroyed the electrical system

The DFS 230s of Gruppe Granit landed on the 'roof' of the fort at Ében-Émael. Although no Belgian (or Franco-British!) strategist could seriously have imagined that the enemy would come from the sky, this large open area of ground running along the deep trench of the canal had been partially lined with obstacles such as stakes and barbed wire. ROBA

and the fort was soon plunged into total darkness. Telephone communications were cut off between HQ and the gutted cupolas. Major Jean Jottrand, commander of Ében-Émael, issued orders that could not be carried out. Patrols sent to the hot spots were 'picked off' in the narrow dark corridors by the fire of airborne troops who had penetrated the fortress and dug in. Unlike their opponents, Ében-Émael's gunners had not been trained in hand-to-hand combat and had to withdraw. Suddenly, the Ju 87s of StG 2 intervened, their attacks facilitated by the 'message panels' deployed by the parachutists on the glacis. The fort literally shook under the explosions of the Stuka bombs. Shortly afterwards, as the ground forces approached the canal, long-range guns 'sprayed' the fort.

The next day, after 24 hours of uncertainty, procrastination and abortive attempts at counter-attack, the garrison capitulated. Ében-Émael, the 'impregnable fortress', had fallen. Rudolf Witzig's group achieved this astonishing success with only six killed and 20 wounded (some of them seriously). The dead were initially buried on the fort's roof. It seems that all the glider pilots in the Granit group were unharmed.

THE BRIDGE AT VROENHOVEN

According to the report by the leader of the Gruppe Beton, Oblt Gerhard Schlacht: "Attack led

Ogfr Pilz, left, probably recounting his flight to Ében-Émael. He was forced to land near Cologne after his tow cable snapped, before leaving again with Witzig's group. Pilz wears the ribbon of the EK I awarded for this mission. ROBA

After the battle — a Storch has landed close to one of the armoured cupolas. MEYER VIA STIPDONK

The glacis roof of the fortress dotted with gliders. In order to come to a stand as quickly as possible on landing, twisting barbed wire around the gliders' skids proved a quick and effective solution. An image that highlights how the combat teams brought in by DFS 230 arrived 'together' as groups, whereas individual paratroopers would be widely dispersed.

DFS 230 on the roof of the fort — uncamouflaged and displaying no national markings.

In the village of Ében-Émael, the 'surviving' gliders are collected together to be dismantled and repatriated. They must have been few in number. VIA IAN TANNAHILL

by five officers and 129 men. Take-off at 0430 from Ostheim with 11 gliders. During the well-lit flight, Obj Kempa's machine was lost due to a broken cable. Landing at Hottdorf. For some unexplained reason, the gliders fly over Dutch territory at a height of 2,000m. Separation of the gliders took place between the German border and Maastricht…Powerful Dutch flak was encountered but, thanks to the skill of the pilots, no aircraft were hit.

"The bridge was clearly visible and the critical task was to prevent the soldiers on duty from blowing it up. At an altitude of around 100m, the ten gliders came under machine-gun and rifle fire. Obj Stolzewszki's aircraft took a shell and crashed from a height of 12m. Three men were seriously injured and were unable to fight. Ofw Hoffmann's aircraft did not land near the bunker as planned but fell 100m away into a ditch. Three men were killed. It must have been the DFS 230 piloted by Gefreiter Walter Daum who was killed in the fight."

According to J-L Lhoest, the soldiers of the 18th Regiment 'Ligne de garde' on guard near the bridge were alerted by Dutch anti-aircraft fire. Groups of aircraft suddenly appeared flying towards the canal. Flying at varying heights, they reached the canal between Lanaye and Briegden and then the formations, seemingly obeying a general order, broke up in all directions. "Look," shouted a corporal, "they've been hit..."

And indeed, many aircraft were slowly coming down, some even flying over the canal. Some soldiers realised they were being attacked by strange unmotorised aircraft when the gliders began to land. They opened fire but already seven aircraft were landing simultaneously on the west bank. One of the gliders touched down 50m north of the shelter. Still believing it to be a downed aircraft, a marshal rushed towards it to capture the crew. He was badly injured in the leg by a burst of machine-gun fire. Soldiers emerged from the gliders and immediately fired on the Belgians.

Shortly afterwards, Stukas bombed the area around the bridge, adding to the confusion. The two small bunkers (one of which housed the bridge destruction mechanism) were overwhelmed. Within the hour, the small group led by Koch received reinforcements and supplies by parachute from Ju 52s. When the Heer forces came to support the airborne troops, the Germans had seven dead before evacuating 24 wounded: the price to pay for capturing the Vroenhoven bridge intact. One hundred and forty-seven Belgian soldiers were killed and 200-300 others captured. The Panzers were able to cross the canal. By 10am they were already in Riemst, a long way on the other bank.

A line of graves with a DFS 230 would seem to place this scene near Vroenhoven (Gruppe Beton).

VELDWEZELT

According to the report by Oblt Gustav Altmann, leading Gruppe Stahl: "On 10 May 1940, nine gliders took off from Ostheim and one from Butzweilerhof at around 0430. Everything went smoothly, with the planes following the 'searchlight route' and separating from the gliders when they reached an altitude of 2,300m to 2,600m. The Dutch towns were not obscured, which made it easier for the gliders to fly, but the Gruppe Beton had pushed too far and, alerted by the flak, we came under fire near Maastricht. As we were flying at a high altitude, it was ineffective.

"The target was well spotted, but heavy flak and machine-gun fire greeted us. One glider took a direct hit that destroyed part of its left wing. The pilot, Uffz Stuhr, also suffered a head injury. The aircraft crashed from a height of about 10m and some of its occupants were put out of action. The other gliders landed near their assigned points, but the one belonging to Ellersiek's troop overturned and one soldier suffered two broken arms."

According to J-L Lhoest, the Belgian soldiers of the 2nd Carabinieri present near the Veldwezelt bridge were also surprised by these strange aircraft. Near the bridge, a sergeant was chatting with some soldiers when the planes whirled around. They said: "Our attention was caught by the unusual appearance of these aircraft orbiting over the canal at our height. None of us could tell what they were because we had never seen anything like them. We watched, intrigued, with a strange feeling of foreboding in the pit of our stomachs..."

Once again, the nine gliders landed in perfect synchronicity. Three to the north of the road, five to the south and one further west. As soon as they hit the ground, the airborne men leapt out of their machines, firing from all barrels. Here, the man responsible for destroying the bridge would have

Gruppe Stahl pilot Wilhelm Fulda at the controls of his DFS 230 as 'immortalised' by the famous portrait painter Wolf Wilrich. His Fallschirmjäger 'Springerhelm' helmet would provide some head protection during a rough landing.

tried to light the fuse but was unable to succeed given the speed of the assault. The group of Arpke pioneers immediately rushed into the bunkers, blowing them up (often with their occupants).

During the fighting, paratroopers transported in Ju 52s came to support their comrades and the reinforced Gruppe Stahl held out until the early afternoon, before infantrymen reached the scene. Eight paras were killed and 30 others wounded. One hundred and fifteen Belgian soldiers were killed and several hundred captured. Thirty-five civilians were killed (mainly by bombs), with another 45 wounded as a result of the proximity of houses.

CANNE

Canne was the least successful of the airborne operations on 10 May—if not to say a failure. However, as Lhoest put it: "The capture of the Canne bridge was the weak point of the airborne operations on the Albert Canal. The risk of failure was apparent. It was decided to go ahead, even though the Canne bridge seemed to be less important than the other two. What made Canne different from the other bridges was its impassable

A DFS 230 being dismantled at Veldwezelt.

terrain. The bridge was 4m above the level of the canal, whose western bank was inaccessible to gliders. Since the operation had to be carried out at all costs, the number of gliders would have had to be greatly increased. But this too was unfeasible given the conditions at the start in Cologne."

The more likely probability was the shortage of available DFS 230s as a result of the relatively low numbers of gliders constructed.

However, the report by the head of Gruppe Eisen, Lt Martin Schächter, begins rather positively: "On 10 May 1940, at around 0230, Sturmgruppe Eisen took off from Butzweilerhof in the dark in ten gliders. The formation followed the lit route and all the gliders separated at an altitude of 2,500m, except for the glider of the first group (Czerwinska) which broke away at 2,000m and was unable to land at the set location."

The gliders also came under fire from Dutch flak but suffered no losses. The Ju 52 pilots also appear to have towed the DFS 230s a little too far and the Eisen group arrived at the target a little later than scheduled. With the other three groups already engaged in combat, Major Jottrand, commander of Ében-Émael ordered the bridge to be blown up immediately (this structure was in fact part of the fortress). As the nine gliders barely touched the ground, Gruppe Eisen's target was blown up. Machine-gun fire set alight one of the DFS 230s, which was still some 30m above the ground. Its pilot nevertheless managed to land and his passengers disembarked. Given the lack of surprise, the Canne airborne suffered more severe losses than those of the other three groups. Bad luck also affected the reinforcements: when the Ju 52 dropped 25 paratroopers an hour later, at least half were wiped out by enemy fire.

The following day, the airborne troops were relieved by ground troops. While more than 200 Belgian soldiers were killed and another 200 captured, the airborne troops lost 22 of their own, including a glider pilot, Uffz Berthold Seele. Twenty-six Germans were reported wounded and there was even one missing person... who was found wounded but alive when Dunkirk fell at the end of May. For reasons unknown, Seele's body was repatriated and buried in Hanover-Recklingen.

Despite the destruction of one of the bridges, the successful operations on the Albert Canal were immediately given a high profile by German propaganda, which has been echoed to this day in publications, articles and films, often in glowing terms. Some 400 men transported by 42 gliders had neutralised 'the most powerful fortress' in Europe and enabled the Panzer divisions to advance rapidly into Belgium, thus probably saving the ambitious Fall Gelb if not the entire Blitzkrieg.

The participants were showered with medals. As early as 15 May, with Fall Gelb in full swing, Adolf Hitler received a number of airborne leaders at his campaign HQ, including Walter Kiess, pilot in Gruppe Beton and presented several Knight's Crosses. Student also received the Ritterkreuz, while almost all the other combatants were awarded the EK I (Iron Cross 1st Class).

During the fighting, two pilots were killed (even though most of them stayed out of the fighting) and it is likely that two or three others suffered serious injuries that sidelined them from the flying personnel.

The intact gliders were retrieved and dismantled over the next few days. Of the 42 machines involved, around 20 were recovered in a condition that allowed them to be put back into service. However, the small number of machines available meant that such a feat could not be repeated. Perhaps not surprisingly then, the 10 May 'coup de main' was the only glider operation mounted during the Westfeldzug.

There were plans to attempt another raid, this time in Scandinavia. On 27 May 1940 some 21 DFS 230s, towed by Ju 52s, departed Hildesheim for Aalborg (Denmark). These aircraft from 17./KG z. b.V. 5 then flew to Drontheim (Norway) on 1 June, from where they were to have flown to Narvik to deliver ammunition and supplies to the beleaguered German troops. The pilots wore merchant navy seamen's uniforms so that, if need be, they could cross the Swedish border and claim to be survivors of ships sunk by the British. Given their status as 'non-combatants', they would not have been interned but sent back to the Reich, which is partly true since, although they were part of the military air force, these specialist pilots had to take care to avoid direct engagements. Because of the bad weather and the rapid withdrawal of the Franco-British expeditionary force, this risky mission (probably more suicidal than that of the Albert Canal) was finally cancelled. Shortly afterwards, all the pilots returned to Hildesheim.

As author Jean-Louis Roba put it: "The Albert Canal had suddenly brought into sharp focus the offensive use by the Luftwaffe of combat gliders, even though they were initially intended for transporting cargoes. However, for many authors, this 'coup de main' has rather overshadowed the other successful combat deployments of the DFS 230."

The success of the operation highlighted the value of the glider arm, and led to an increase in production of the DFS 230. By the end of the year, some 455 DFS 230 gliders had been constructed according to the QM General reports. The problem for the Germans was that pilot training lagged behind – the assault in Belgium had only been possible by the drafting in of 'civilian' instructors to fly the DFS 230s into combat.

ÉBEN-ÉMAEL DFS 230 PILOTS

Gruppe Granit: Bräutigam, Bredenbeck, Distelmeier, Kraft, Lange, Pilz, Raschke, Scheidhauer, Schulze, Supper and Ziller.

Gruppe Beton: Daum (KIA), Foltmer, Gehrke, Hempel, Jödike, Kiess, Krusewitz, Oeltjen (?), Pfitzner, Smyczek and Stern. Oblt Walter Kiess commanded the glider wing of Sturmabteilung Koch, 17./KG z.b.V. 5.

Gruppe Eisen: Hartebrodt, Noske, Over, Rieger, Schedalke, Schikowski, Schweigmann, Seele (KIA), Specht and Winkler.

Gruppe Stahl: Bösebeck, Egner, Flucke, Fulda, Opitz, Schubert, Staubach, Stoffel, Stuhr and Wienberg.

Six men of Gruppe Granit. Otto Bräutigam is third from the right. Along with other civilian glider pilots, he was brought in to the Ében-Émael attack force to make up the shortfall of qualified DFS 230 pilots. They were given uniforms and low ranks but had no combat training at the time of the raid and once on the ground would help guard prisoners and tend the wounded. VIA GREG WAY

On 15 May 1940, at his Felsennest HQ in Rodert (near Münstereifel), Adolf Hitler welcomed the airborne troops who had fought on the Albert Canal on 10 May and awarded several Ritterkreuze. From left to right: Lt Egon Delica (RK on 12.5.40), Oblt Rudolf Witzig (RK on 10.5.40), Hptm Walther Koch (RK on 10.5.40), Oblt Otto Zierach (RK on 15.10.40), Adolf Hitler, Lt d. R. Helmut Ringler (RK on 15.5.40), Lt d. R. Joachim Meissner (RK on 12.5.40), Oblt and glider commander Walter Kiess (RK on 12.5.40), Oblt Gustav Altmann (RK on 12.5.40) and Dr Rolf Jäger (RK on 13.5.40).

Seen here after Ében-Émael, two notable glider pilots — Erwin Ziller and Wilhelm Fulda — were photographed with their recently awarded EK I. Another 'world champion' glider flyer, Ziller was killed while testing a Horten flying wing on 18 February 1945. Fulda was awarded the Ritterkreuz in 1941 and survived the war. VIA ROBA

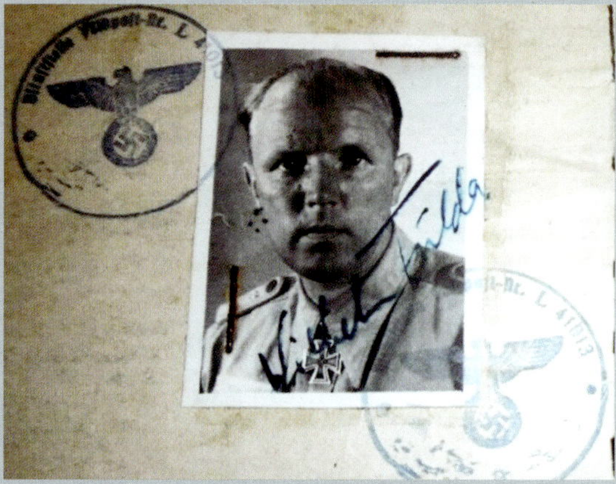

Glider pilot Wilhelm Fulda.

Awarded the Knight's Cross for his role in Operation 'Steel, Concrete, Iron, Granite', Egon Delica joined the Stab of LLG 1 in early 1942. He then became Staffelführer of 4./LLG 2 in Nancy (10 October 1942). At the end of the war, he led the II. Battalion/Fallschirm-Jäger-Regiment 19.

PILOT PROFILE — WILHELM FULDA

Wilhelm Fulda (left) seen with Karl-Heinz Lange following the Ében-Émael /Albert Canal mission. Both are wearing their EK I. Lange, who sustained injuries and was recovering in hospital, has his on his pyjama top. Later on in the war, Lange was the 'brains' behind the idea of a specialist Luftwaffe bridge destruction unit — Sonderstaffel Einhorn. VIA IAN TANNAHILL

Born in Antwerp on May 21, 1909, Wilhelm Fulda joined up on 1 November 1935. Like most on the Ében-Émael raid, he had learnt to fly in the NSFK. After completion of his glider pilot training he was assigned to the 17./Kampfgruppe zbV 5. In his first combat mission with Sturmabteilung Koch (assault battalion Koch) he landed a DFS 230 on the roof of the Belgian fort at Ében-Émael. For this feat he was awarded the Iron Cross 1st class (Eisernes Kreuz 1. Klasse) on 13 May 1940.

Fulda was awarded the Knight's Cross for his actions as a glider pilot during the attack on the Corinthian Isthmus, Greece. His award is dated 22 June 1941. There is no record of Fulda having participated in the landings on Crete. From 4 September 1942 until 4 February 1943 he led the Go 242-equipped 1./Schleppstaffel of Luftlandegeschwader 1 (1st Air Landing Wing). During early 1943 he retrained on Fw 190 fighters, transferring to the single-engine night fighter force ('Wilde Sau') in late 1943, firstly as StaKa with 9./JG 301 (November 1943) before being appointed Gruppenkommandeur of II./JG 301 in January 1944.

During the summer of 1944 the 35-year old Fulda was appointed Staffelkapitän of 5.(Sturm)/JG 4 – a Fw 190-equipped Sturmgruppe serving in the 'bomber destroyer' role in the so-called Reichsverteidigung, the 'defence of the Reich', whose pilots signed an 'affidavit' pledging to 'ram' enemy bombers if necessary. However Fulda departed this unit before II./JG 4 flew their first 'Sturm' sortie in September. On 28 August 1944, Fulda was named Kommandeur of I./JG 302. In late November 1944 he moved back to gliders of a sort, being appointed to command I. Gruppe of JG 400 operating the rocket-powered Me 163 in Brandis. From there he volunteered for Herrmann's Sonderkommando Elbe, a 'ramming' unit which flew a single mission during April 1945 against USAF bomber formations. Fulda was credited with the destruction of a single four-engine bomber. He died in Hamburg on 8 August, 1977.

Fulda is seen here at a 'reunion' for NSFK Ritterkreuz holders during 1943. Note on his tunic, directly beneath his EK I, his glider pilot Segelflieger Abzeichen (probably in Gold) with the three 'gull wings'. SAINTES VIA ROBA

PILOT PROFILE – RUDOLF 'RUDI' OPITZ

'Rudi' Opitz was born 9 August 1910 in Landeshut, Silesia. Between 1927 and 1934 he trained and was employed as a carpenter and joiner, specialising in wooden aircraft construction. In 1934 he became a glider instructor with the RRG on the Wasserkuppe and then instructor with the DFS. Having achieved numerous awards for gliding, Opitz was one of the three original instructors to teach the first German military glider pilots to fly at the DFS.

On 9 November 1939 he enlisted with the rank of Flieger in the Luftwaffe, served as a chief glider instructor in the glider corps (to around August 1940), prior to being detached to the Sturmabteilung Koch. On 10 May 1940 he piloted a DFS 230 in the attack on Ében-Émael, was awarded the EK I and promoted to Feldwebel.

During the summer of 1941, Opitz served as a test pilot at the Erprobungsstelle Rechlin and was involved in the development of the Me 163 rocket fighter. He performed the first flight with the Me 163 B on 24 June 1943. By January he was one of the chief instructors in the Me 163 test and training unit, Erprobungskommando 16. In April he was promoted to Oberleutnant before being named Staka 1./JG 400.

He survived several crash-landings at the controls of the Me 163 rocket fighters – flying Me 163 B V33 (GH+IL) he made an emergency landing at Bad Zwischenahn due to engine trouble and crash-landed at Lärz in Me 163 B V29 (GH+IH). During July 1944 he was promoted to Oblt.

On 14 October 1944 he held the role of acting Kommandeur of I./JG 400 for four weeks, prior to being named Kdr. II./JG 400 during December 1944. On 1 January 1945 he was awarded the DKiG (German Cross in Gold, usual precursor to the Ritterkreuz). As a Hauptmann in JG 400, he was WIA in the crash landing of a burning Me 163 at Husum and hospitalized with several broken bones. Post-war he settled in Australia and died on 1 May 2010.

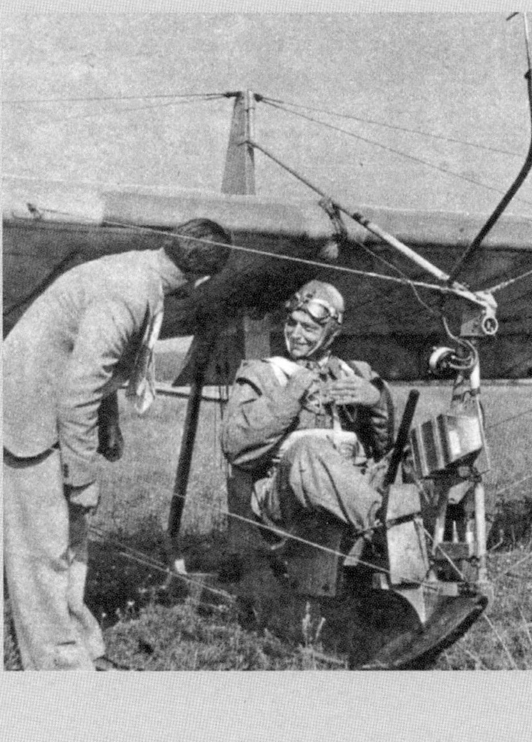

'Rudi' Opitz seen pre-war at the controls of an SG 38 sailplane on the Wasserkuppe. VIA IAN TANNAHILL

3

LUFTLANDEGESCHWADER 1 AND 'SEA LION' PREPARATIONS

THE IMPACT of the use of gliders at the Albert Canal was bound to prompt the Luftwaffe to organise and strengthen this new combat arm. In late July 1940, Luftlandegeschwader 1 ('airborne assault wing 1' or LLG 1) was established and initially comprised two Gruppen. This was achieved by splitting Kiess' augmented 17/.KG z.b.V. 5 into two Gruppen redesignated as:

* I./LLG 1 based in Hildesheim (Kommandeur: Major Dr Walter Kiess)
* II./LLG 1 in Halberstadt (Kommandeur: Hptm Arnold Willerding).

Obstlt Gustav Wilke was named Kommodore of the new Geschwader. Although I. and II./LLG 1 had their own status, they were initially assigned to 7. Fliegerdivision under General Kurt Student. However, Kommodore Wilke was a Ju 52 pilot. He led a transport unit (KG z.b.V. 11) during the Westfeldzug, having been awarded the Ritterkreuz in May.

Hptm Arnold Willerding had served with KG z.b.V. 2 before the war then took charge of the Segelflugschule (gliding school) at Braunschweig-Waggum. These two officers were certainly competent, but their careers as 'transporter' pilots contrasted with the propaganda vision – glider leaders were supposedly so-called 'Draufgänger' (go-getters) launched into battle.

A third Gruppe, III./LLG 1, was formed in August 1940 at Waggum, the Braunschweig (Brunswick) airfield, with Major Richard Kupschuss at its head. This former transport pilot had led the FFS C 15 since January 1940. The appointment of another 'school' commander confirms that the main aim of LLG 1 was to train glider pilots and, secondarily, to imbue them with fighting spirit.

To bolster its ranks, the Luftwaffe exploited the existing small pool of young glider pilots who had flown gliders pre-war. Young men (born 1920 to 1922) who had been in the Hitlerjugend or NSFK were called up to the new Geschwader. They had the appropriate certificates and already had some flying experience. Entry was not automatic, of course, and applicants had to undergo training in twin-seat machines at schools such as Trebbin or Ith before moving on to the schools in Goslar, Halberstadt or Hildesheim. Around 30 trainees were assigned to each Gruppe of LLG 1. Ground-based combat training – 'Erdkampfausbildung' – followed in early 1941.

The short-range recce Henschel Hs 126 was virtually obsolescent by 1940 and would take no part in the Battle of Britain — but several hundred of this type were deployed during Barbarossa. With transport capacity impacted by the demands placed on the Junkers Ju 52 fleet, the Hs 126 saw widespread service as a tug to tow the DFS 230.

Since the Fl.Schule der Lw (S) 1 could no longer occupy the overcrowded Waggum airfield, it moved to Neuhausen (East Prussia). With Kommandeur Willerding having left to lead II./LLG 1, the school received a new director in the person of Obstlt Ludwig Reeps.

The development of the Luftwaffe combat glider arm was, as might have been expected, hampered by a lack of resources. The Luftwaffe was struggling to recover from the fighting of 1940, having lost hundreds of aircraft and thousands of aircrew over Western Europe, and was also trying to prepare for the invasion of the USSR. Gliders were well down the 'pecking order' during this period of rebuilding and were bound to suffer as a result. Henschel Hs 126s (already considered partially obsolete) were regularly used as tugs in place of the Ju 52s, which were retained for other, higher priority tasks. It would even appear that one or two Staffeln of LLG 1 did not have any tow aircraft at the time. The Geschwader therefore had to rely on the goodwill of its counterparts to train its DFS 230 pilots.

SEA LION

After the fall of France at the end of June 1940, Britain stood alone. However, the Wehrmacht – exhausted, even surprised by the rapid

A snow-bound DFS 230. JAMES V. CROW COLLECTION

Junkers Ju 52s of LLG 1 displaying the Geschwader emblem. MEYER/STIPDONK

A 'Kette' of DFS 230 gliders hooked up to their Ju 52 tugs. This unusual view has been taken from the tailwheel of the tug. VIA PAUL STIPDONK

Close-up of the tail wheel tow cable anchor on the Ju 52 tug. This 'Schleppkupplung' developed by Junkers (Ju 3000) was prone to twisting, which could lead to an 'Auskupplung' or 'disengagement'. VIA PAUL STIPDONK

victories achieved on the continent – did not have the resources to attempt an invasion of England, due to a lack of suitable shipping. Despite what can still be read elsewhere, 'Sea Lion' was never a real plan. According to some, the large-scale air actions over England (the 'Battle of Britain', then the 'Blitz') ostensibly designed to 'clear the skies' over England, were as much about creating political pressure for peace as they were a serious attempt to 'cow' the British militarily. Whichever way they are viewed, these attempts largely failed.

It is said that shortly after the French surrender, in the wake of the success on the Albert Canal, the German high command planned to drop paratroopers and gliders as quickly as possible around Folkestone, Kent, and create a bridgehead for landings in southern England. Such an operation would have turned into a massacre for the Luftwaffe and its slow Ju 52s. RAF Fighter Command had carefully husbanded the deployment of its modern Spitfires, largely keeping them in the UK. In addition, by the end of May, British army officials were receiving Ultra reports – decryptions of Luftwaffe messages sent by radio with Enigma machine encoding – within 24 hours. Notwithstanding the fact that, at that time, the Luftwaffe had only around 30 gliders and trained pilots... nowhere near enough to send a credible force across the Channel!

The glider pilots nevertheless trained for 'Seelöwe'. Uffz Franz Lankenau, a Ju 52 pilot with II./KG z.b.V. 1, was assigned to this task: "In mid-August, the entire Gruppe was sent to Posen. The DFS 230 gliders which had been employed with such success at Ében-Émael were being assembled here. Our Ju 52s were fitted with tow hooks and accessories at the tailwheel and our training in towing gliders began very quickly. The training was based on the experiences that had already proved successful in the West – an approach at high altitude in darkness, releasing the gliders for a long silent approach that would catch the enemy by surprise at dawn.

"We started off alone so that the glider pilot and the Ju 52 crew could 'trust' each other. Once this was done, we were able to fly in formation. Suddenly, in mid-September, the order came to fly to Laon where an advanced detachment was already present. But on 17 September, on an intermediate stop in Stendal, this order was cancelled. So we went to Parchim where we stayed until April 1941. Training resumed intensively. On completion of their training, the DFS 230 pilots had to take off with gliders loaded with sand-bags and land at night on unlit airfields. I made one such flight in one of these gliders with its primitive instruments and had to admire the pilot's ability to land perfectly in the designated area. During one of these flights, a glider crashed and the pilot was killed. As 'Seelöwe' was not launched, the gliders were moved and our crews underwent further blind flying training..."

In the end, this reinforced training period was superfluous. However, the temporary and then definitive postponement of 'Seelöwe' did not impact the development of the Luftwaffe glider force, which was then in full swing.

Another operation was envisaged but then cancelled: 'Felix', the invasion of the island of Gibraltar, which required the use of gliders from LLG 1 and sappers from the 51st Engineer Battalion – the same battalion that had contributed to the capture of the fort at Ében-Émael. Despite the Spanish government's earnest desire to see such an attack carried out and to 'recover' this strategic British possession blocking the Mediterranean, the Caudillo Franco had to give up on assisting the Third Reich with this operation, given the disastrous situation in his country, which had just emerged from a bloody civil war. 'Felix' was quickly buried. Once again, this was a good thing for the airborne troops, as such an invasion would have generated numerous messages that could easily have been deciphered by Ultra, and the German paratroopers would have almost certainly have encountered stiff opposition on their arrival.

A DFS 230 seen on the airfield at Braunschweig Waggum. Pilot training on the DFS 230 had begun here in February 1940. Students joining the Luftwaffe and already holding the glider proficiency 'C' class badge were discreetly 'invited' to train as military glider pilots. They required just four weeks of intensive training to be considered competent on the DFS 230.

Training on the DFS 230 at LLG 1 in Posen 1941. VIA PAUL STIPDONK

Langendiebach, DFS 230 S1+A16 with trainee pilots. VIA PAUL STIPDONK

In training for Seelöwe (Sea Lion), II./KG z.b.V. 1 carried out formation flights with DFS 230s.

As a rule of thumb, the glider pilot maintained an altitude some 5-10m higher than that of the towing aircraft to minimise the impact of the tug's 'bow wave', described as being 'like water-skiing behind a speedboat'. The turbulent air was considerably reduced according to the length of the towing cable. A single Ju 52 could tow two DFS 230s as here, albeit with difficulty.

A DFS 230 behind a He 45 tug — a shorter tow rope required increased attention on the part of the glider pilot and gave him less 'freedom' of movement.

Pre-war trials were held using a short rigid tow-bar, the so-called Starrschlepp, as one solution to the problem of tow cables snapping.

As the number of gliders in service grew — putting strain on the numbers of available tugs — some ad hoc solutions for towing the DFS 230 were sought. Here a DFS 230 is flown off the ground by an antique Czech Letov Š 328 biplane. The Germans used captured Š-328s both as trainers and in the night attack role on the Eastern Front in the winter of 1942—43, while some of the 400 produced went to their allies, Bulgaria and Slovakia.

THE DFS 230

A brief description of the DFS 230 A-1's main assemblies is provided in the type's technical manual as follows:

* **Fuselage:** steel tubular framework covered with canvas. Pilot cockpit with folding plexiglass canopy. Passenger compartment with side windows. One door on the left

side behind the wing for boarding/disembarking. Possibility of increasing the space in the rear section.

* **Landing gear:** wheels released after take-off. Landing is on a skid.
* **Wings:** wooden, partially covered with canvas. 'Brake flaps' on the upper surface [wing construction was fairly complex comprising no fewer than 400 ribs and some 12,000 individual parts].
* **Tailplane and horizontal stabiliser:** both made of plywood and partially covered with canvas. Trim fitted.

The type handbook also adds a few details about the presence of two first-aid kits placed at the rear of the fuselage, as well as the possibility of instrument or 'blind' flights.

Though they were externally very similar, the DFS 230 went through several variants:

* The A-1 was used at the start of the war and featured jettisonable take-off wheels, a single-piece canopy and only one entrance door. The pilot and first five men at the front had to embark through the cockpit. The rear four entered through a hatch aft of the wing and sat on a 'communal' bench facing rearwards. Each passenger had a chair brace to lean back onto and to hold onto in front.
* The A-2, which soon followed, featured a windscreen and a rudder trim tab and a right side rear door. A triangular 'folding' section behind the cockpit was incorporated which opened up to facilitate entry and exit.

Rare view of a DFS 230 with the upper wing 'brake flaps' deployed. Note the undercarriage has not been jettisoned. VIA PAUL STIPDONK

* The B-1, produced from the beginning of 1941, had dual controls and was intended for training glider pilots.
* The B-2, also with dual controls, was a front-line aircraft.
  A-1s could become A-2s by simply changing the rudder, while A-types could also be transformed into B-types as required. Official loss lists typically only mention the glider and very rarely its sub-type.
* The C-1, with an elongated fuselage, was equipped with a braking parachute and, according to some sources, braking rockets in the nose. It also had an additional fuselage door added forward of the left wing.

The DFS 230 C series featured an additional loading door forward of the port wing and a slightly wider fuselage. These features were not 'definitive', as the A and B versions also received a braking parachute around 1943.

PRODUCTION

Based on available documents, production figures were as follows:

-**1939:** 28 aircraft
-**1940:** 455
-**1941:** 1,020 (Robert Hartwig: 308; Bücker: 180; Gotha: 32; Erla: 178; BMM (Prague): 322)
-**1942:** 74
-**1944:** 14

According to the monthly 'C-Amts' reports, no DFS 230s were built in 1943. Some 375 A-1/A-2 variants were produced. The major manufacturer of the type was Hartwig's in Sonneberg (Thuringia) although at least five manufacturers were involved in DFS 230 construction. Ten DFS 230s were sold to Italy in 1940 and a further 50 in 1943. The DFS 230 was also used by the Romanians who purchased 15 in 1942 and 23 in 1943. Some of the Romanian gliders were used as transport at the front.

ARMAMENT

In a 1942 memo to Göring, Student emphasised that significant advances had been made in the field of combat gliders. One of the major 'vulnerabilities' of airborne troops was how lightly armed they were in comparison to regular formations. The DFS 230 was not initially equipped with offensive armament but Student had ordered his DFS 230 glider force to be fitted with one fixed and one moveable MG so that the "combat gliders can suppress enemy defences through their own means". These were first carried for offensive operations, probably from the date of the Corinth mission in May 1941.

An MG 34 was attached to the right forward fuselage of the DFS 230. Once the glider came to a stand, the gunner behind the pilot could unstrap it and set it up. Subsequently, DFS 230s carrying personnel were also equipped with the roof-mounted MG 15 (above and to the rear of the cockpit), enabling the landing area to be covered even as the glider was coming in on its approach.

Characteristics	Type A-B	Type C
Wingspan	21.98m	22.28m
Fuselage width	0.70m	1m
Length	11m	11.24m
Height	2.74m	2.74m
Wing area	41.26m^2	42.07m^2
Empty weight	780/830kg	940kg
Load	1,200kg	1,200kg
Max tow speed	185km/h	260km/h
Landing speed	87km/h	88km/h
Diving speed	290km/h	290/kmh

Ladeplan für DFS 230

Verwendungs- und Beanspruchungsgruppe: P 3

Pos.	Benennung	Verwendungszwecke I Zugtrupp	II MG-Trupp	III Schützentrupp
	Leergewicht	783 kg	783 kg	783 kg
	zusätzl. Ausrüstung *)	32	32	32
	Rüstgewicht	815	815	815
	Fahrwerk (abwerfbar)	40	40	40
	Zuladung:			
1	Besatzung	70—100	70—100	70—100
2	"	70—100	70—100	70—100
3	"	70—100	70—100	70—100
4	"	70—100	70—100	70—100
5	"	70—100	70—100	70—100
6	"	70—100	70—100	70—100
7	"	70—100	70—100	70—100
8	"	70 100	70—100	70—100
9	"	70—100	70—100	70—100
10	"	70—100	70—100	70—100
11	6 Gewehre	23	23	23
12	6 Munitionskästen (voll)	—	50	50
13	1 schweres MG	—	36	—
14	1 leichtes MG	—	—	13
15	2 Funk-Kästen	35	—	—
	Fluggewicht (mit Fahrwerk)	1913	1964	1941 kg

Max. Fluggew.-Schwerpunktsvorlage: — 174 mm vor Hauptspant = 27,3% to
" " " — 15 mm " " = 33 % to

Anmerkung: Höchstzulässiges Fluggewicht 2100 kg. Bei Alleinflug sind 60 kg Ballast auf Sitz 2 mitzunehmen. Schwere Insassen haben bei voller Besatzung die Sitze Nr. 2, 3, 4, 5 usw. zu belegen. to = Flügeltiefe in Symmetrie-Ebene (2,8 m). Vord. Punkt von to liegt — 0,94 m vor Hauptspant.

*) siehe Beladevorschrift.

Load plan for a DFS 230 in passenger transport configuration (nine men in addition to the pilot). The rear-most set of seats could be removed to augment load carrying capacity.

The DFS 230 A-2 was equipped with a rudder trim tab.

A view of the 'communal' bench seating.

Cockpit of a DFS 230. The control column was shaped "like an elongated tennis racket".

DFS 230 pilot's eye view of the Ju 52 tug. Note (left) the sliding panel in the glazing.

The instrument panel featured a clock and a simple bank of six dials. Note the firing button for the MG 34 on the spade grip. VIA PAUL STIPDONK

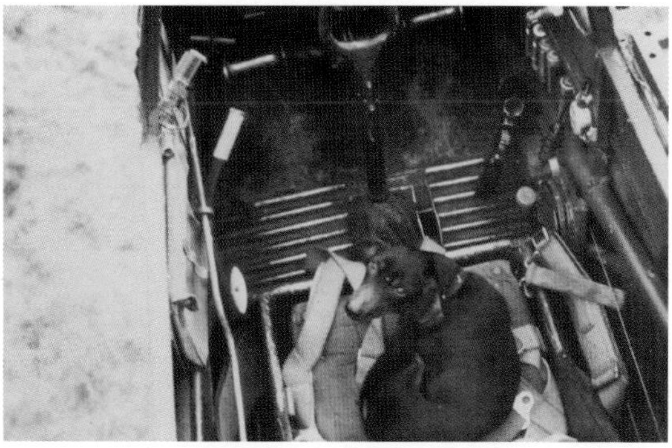

A rare view of the pilot's seat. Note the control levers (right) for the 'braking flaps' mounted in the upper wing surfaces. VIA PAUL STIPDONK

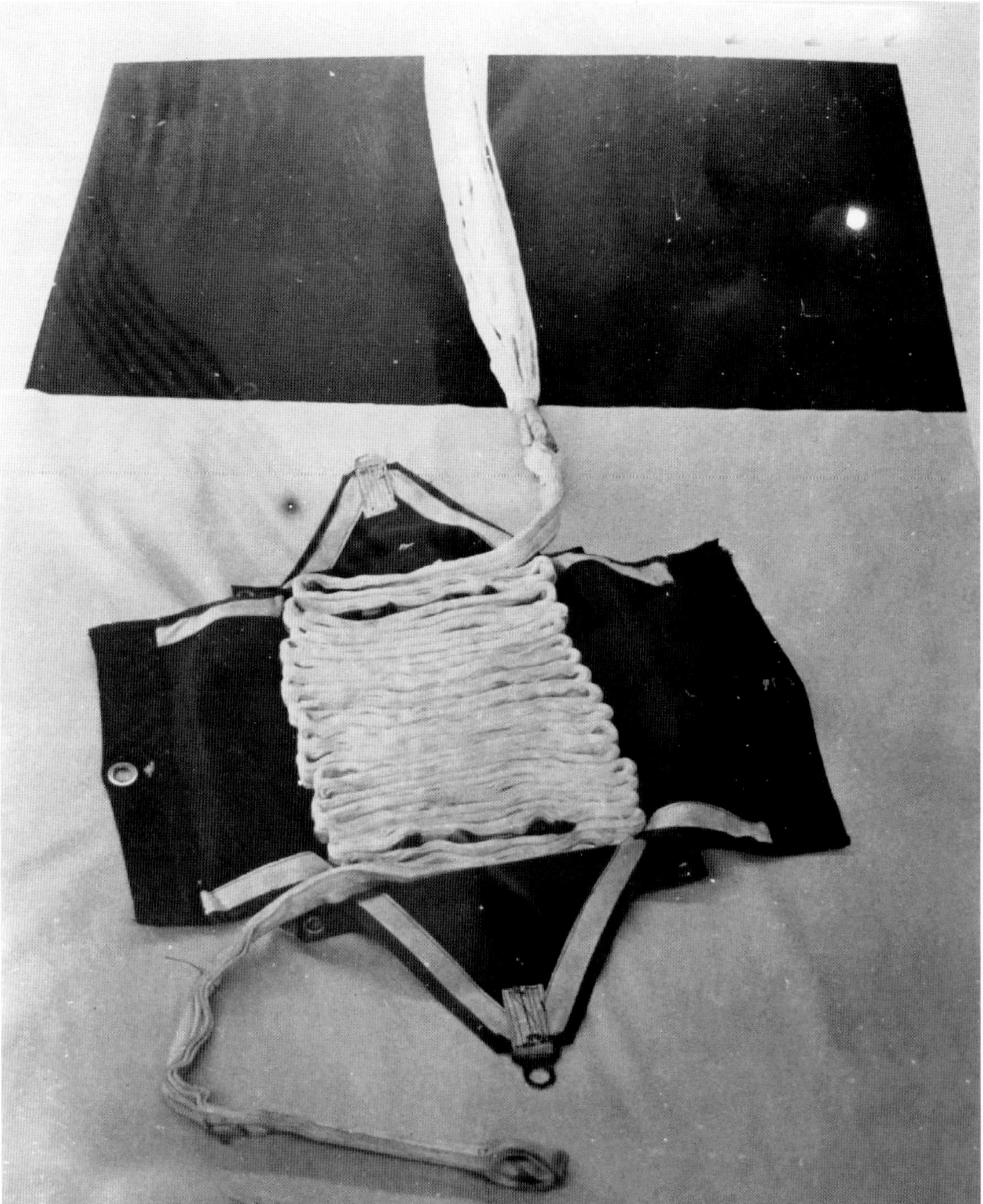

The braking parachute (here folded) was housed at the rear of the DFS. The parachute had a dual purpose — deployed to initiate a steep dive in a 'collared' position and then flared at about 20m altitude to slow the aircraft on landing.

MG 15 machine gun at the rear of the cockpit of a DFS 230, operated by one of the passengers during landing.

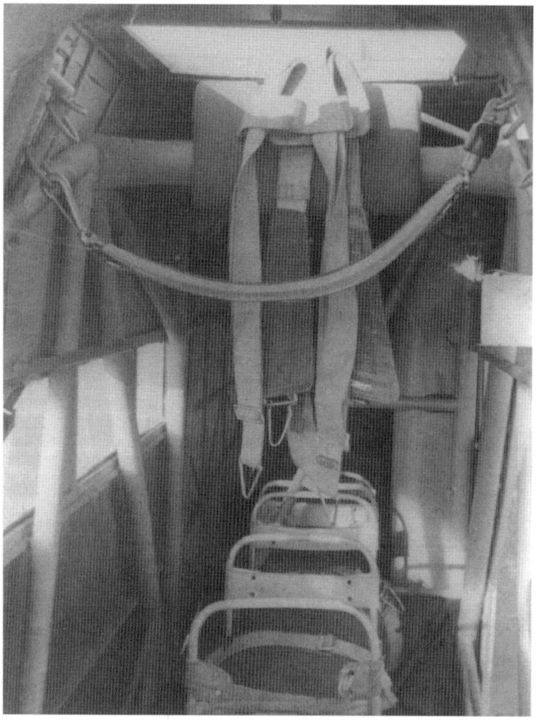

Interior view of a DFS 230 looking towards the rear. Note the opening in the roof for the gunner behind the pilot. His harness and seat strap can be seen.

Late in the war, the C-1 type was fitted with nose-mounted rockets to increase its braking capacity.

4

'MARITA' AND 'MERKUR'

(1) CORINTH

On 6 April 1941, the Wehrmacht launched Operation Marita, the invasion of the Balkans. Yugoslavia having surrendered on the 17th, the Greek troops retreated under the German thrust, while the Commonwealth Expeditionary Force rushed to the embarkation beaches in Attica. When these were within range of Luftwaffe bombers, the evacuation moved to the Peloponnese. For almost 50 years, the isthmus had been separated from the mainland by the Corinth Canal, which played almost the same role as the Albert Canal a year earlier. It represented a major obstacle for an invader keen to make rapid progress in a war of movement. A single bridge crossed this obstacle, the Germans' ideal target. Once in their hands, it would enable them to block the retreat route of the opposing troops while making it easier for their Panzers to cross the canal. It was therefore tempting to repeat the daring glider-borne feat of May 1940.

During the development of 'Marita', the capture of the Corinth Bridge had been given due consideration. Reconnaissance aircraft had taken photos of the bridge from Italy. As early as March 1941, the staff of the 7. Fliegerdivision (then based in Bulgaria) had been informed of the forthcoming operation. Surprised by the rapid withdrawal of the Greek-British forces, those in charge of 'Marita' issued a hasty order to take the structure on 25 April.

According to Ofw Gerhard Raschke, a 'veteran' of the Albert Canal mission, the operation was hurriedly prepared: "In Hildesheim the pilots were assigned for an operation in the Balkans. The train with the flying and ground personnel left Hildesheim and, via Regensburg, travelled along the Danube to Bulgaria. We then reached Count Ignatieff airfield (Plovdiv). The DFS gliders were unloaded from the wagons and reassembled in the hangars. There were between 15 and 20 of them. Around 20 April the pilots were designated: Lt (Franz) Phen, Uffz Mende, Gefr Lassen, Fw (Friedrich) Bredenbeck, Lt Fulda and myself. We did not know our objective. An MG 34 was mounted externally near the cockpit and barbed wire wrapped around the skids of the DFS to increase the braking effect as we reckoned we would have to land on sandy ground."

Three of these six 3./LLG 1 pilots were 'old hands' from the operations in Belgium a year earlier.

"On 25 April in the afternoon, six aircraft were placed on the runway and the DFS 230s were hooked up. We headed for Larissa and overflew Salonika. We flew alone in our aircraft for 400km – no ground crews on board – and, at about 7pm, reached Larissa. The gliders were not tied down but simply parked at the edge of the runway. At about 2200 paratroopers arrived in Ju 52s and at midnight we studied the aerial photos of the Corinth Canal. The Fallschirmpioniere were then divided by aircraft (eight men with one Unteroffizier) and practised embarking and disembarking. On 26 April, at about 0500, everything was ready. The gliders were attached to the Ju 52s and take-offs took place in Kette formation (three planes). The propwash of the Ju 52s kick-up large clouds of dust and the take-off is blind.

"Shortly after leaving the ground, the gliders jettison their landing gear and it was not until they were about 50m above the ground that the pilots could finally see their tugs again. However, it took a few minutes for the second Kette to take to the air, the dust cloud reaching 100m! After making several turns, the formation coalesced. To the right, the summit of Mount Olympus could be seen illuminated by the morning sun. As they flew over the mountain range, the Ju 52s found it difficult to gain altitude due to the turbulence. About 20km from the target, we were flying at 1,200m."

Some 2-3km from the canal, the gliders were released before splitting into two formations. The Kette flying south overflew the canal for a while before landing very close to the target. However, Lt Franz Phen's aircraft collided violently with the bridge ramp. The glider broke in two on impact. The pilot and the medic sitting behind him were ejected. They were killed, as were their eight comrades who remained in the cabin. However, the carcass of the glider and the bodies of its occupants had by chance come down on top of and prevented access to the bridge's manual destruction system.

The five other gliders landed without difficulty at around 0700 in the planned location with perfect timing, using their MG 34s to silence the opposition. Fifty-four paras emerged from the machines, immediately engaging the enemy. The fighting was brief. An Australian infantry company, Greek soldiers and three defensive tanks were neutralised in less than ten minutes. The paratroopers were already running across the bridge when, it is said, a stray bullet hit the explosives, triggering a blast that blew the structure apart. The bridge fell into the canal 50m below, taking with it the Fallschirmjäger who were crossing it. While fighting was raging near the bridge, paras from I. and II. FJR were being dropped by Ju 52s on both sides of the Canal. Six other gliders, piloted by Huber, Wächter, Moser, Neelmeier, Pöhl and Haupt, also landed, this time carrying equipment – including light guns.

As these I./LLG 1 gliders had landed on flat ground, Ju 52s were able to land there and, after unloading, bring Fw Walter Wächter's Kette back to Larissa. Seven more DFS transport sorties were to take place, making it possible to secure the sector.

Given that the aim was to capture the bridge intact, the Corinth operation was a failure. If this had not been the case, it would have been sufficient to send a Staffel of Ju 87s. On the other hand, the failure of the operation can in no way be attributed to the use of gliders since, had fate not intervened, the bridge would have been captured without too many hitches. Nevertheless, the glider force had cut off the retreat route of 12,000 exhausted soldiers of the British Expeditionary Force. Caught between enemy forces coming from the north and the almost impassable canal, they had to surrender.

The Germans suffered around 80 killed and missing and around 150 wounded. Two gliders were destroyed and one pilot killed (Lt Franz Phen). The contribution of the DFS 230 Lastensegler was recognised by the award of the Ritterkreuz (in June 1941) to Lt Wilhelm Fulda, the 'leader' of the second glider section of 3./LLG 1, who had transported the sappers of 3 Fallsch. Pi Btl. 7 to the canal. Once on the ground, Fulda did not stay with his DFS 230 but took an active part in the fighting alongside his passengers. However, he would not participate in the next large scale DFS 230 action – Crete.

'Es wird geschwitzt, geflucht und geschuftet' — there is sweating, cursing and toiling! Loading a DFS 230 fuselage onto a rail wagon.

Taking a breather in Bulgaria. DFS 230s for the Corinth action were reassembled at Plovdiv-Krumovo (Bulgaria) away from prying Allied recce aircraft and where this photo was taken. As it was, thanks to Ultra, Allied commanders probably knew more than their German counterparts about the forthcoming operations. VIA PAUL STIPDONK

Two views of disassembled DFS 230s being hauled on trains.

The Corinth Canal cuts through the Isthmus of Corinth connecting the Gulf of Corinth in the Ionian Sea with the Saronic Gulf in the Aegean Sea, separating the Peloponnese from the Greek mainland. Here the eastern end of the canal is seen from a Ju 52.

A total of 12 DFS 230s landed close to the canal at Corinth in two 'waves' of six. These two gliders were possibly Lastensegler of the second wave. Now a modern resort, the coastal village of Loutraki just to the north of the canal is visible in the background at the foot of the Gerania mountains. via Michael Meyer

This rare view probably depicts a Kette (formation of three) of Schleppzüge glider 'trains' of the Corinth canal assault force en route to the target. VIA PAUL STIPDONK

The Corinth canal assault force came down close to an Allied motorised convoy abandoned on the road and a certain amount of war booty was seized. Note the British Bedford truck serving as ad-hoc transport. VIA MICHAEL MEYER

Ju 52s of I./KG z.b.V. 1 (with 'knight' emblem on the nose) were part of the glider support force. A view of the Lechaio airfield close to the canal and town of Corinth, with what appears to be vehicles of the Allied convoy on the coastal road in the background. VIA PAUL STIPDONK

Ofw Gerhard Raschke at the controls of a DFS 230. Note the canopy emergency jettison lever ('Notabwurf'). Raschke flew a DFS 230 with the Gruppe Granit on the Albert canal operation. After Corinth, Raschke was promoted and served as Ia in the Stab/LLG 1. VIA GREG WAY

(II) EINSATZ KRETA – 'MERKUR'

With the British falling back in disorder to the island of Crete, having been 'pushed off the continent' for a second time, action against the island was regarded as "a fitting conclusion to the Greek campaign" for some German strategists. Hitler's Wehrmacht was about to turn against the Soviet Union, with Operation Barbarossa slated to be launched as soon as possible – but Student's Fliegerkorps had no role in this invasion. Student was keen to deploy his force against one of two targets – Malta or Crete, both strategic objectives that could be taken by a Luftwaffe airborne invasion, something that had never been attempted before. According to one account it was Hitler in person who designated Crete for invasion, the decision taken in late April 1941. The plan was codenamed 'Merkur' – Mercury.

According to the Kommandeur of KG z.b.V 105, Major Reinhard Wenning, the Ju 52 transport and tug units first learnt of the Crete 'operation' in Athens on 14 May 1941. Mercury was an air assault that would be launched by around 700 men landed by DFS 230 with (a planned) 10,000 more dropped by parachute with the aim of seizing the airfields and ports of Maleme/Chania, Rethymnon and Heraklion (from west to east on the northern coast of the island) on the first day. Three assault groups were formed: Gruppe West (codenamed 'Komet') tasked with capturing the airfield at Maleme and the high ground overlooking it (Hill 107), Gruppe Mitte ('Mars') ordered to take Chania, Suda and Rethymnon and Gruppe Ost ('Orion') whose mission was to take the airfield and port of Heraklion, some 75km further east along the coast.

7. Fliegerdivision was fully committed. A number of accounts – both wartime and post-1945 – convey the impression that the skies over Crete on 20 May 1941 were full of gliders. In fact, there were relatively few DFS 230 gliders involved in 'Merkur' as confirmed by this record:

* **Stab 7 Fliegerdivision (General Wilhelm Süssmann):** 5 DFS 230s
* **Stab I./Sturmregiment (Major Walther Koch):** 5
* **1. Kompanie (Oblt Alfred Genz):** 9
* **2. Kompanie (Hptm Gustav Altmann):** 15
* **3. Kompanie (Oblt Baron Wulff von Plessen):** 12
* **4. Kompanie (Oblt Kurt Sarrazin):** 12
* **Kampfgruppe Rgt Stab (Major Franz Braun):** 9
* **Portions of the 1./Fallschirm Art.Abt:** 2

A total of 69 gliders.

This comparatively low number can be explained by the almost insurmountable difficulty of transporting these bulky gliders with their rigid – and therefore 'non-dismantling' – fuselages by train in barely two weeks. The only railway line crossing the Balkans, having suffered greatly from the war, was moreover constantly jammed with heavy traffic. Brought by wagons to Salonika, the glider airframes were reassembled at Sedes airfield before being towed to Tanagra by Ju 52s of I./LLG 1. Topolia and Tanagra were the assembly and take-off fields for Gruppe West and Gruppe Ost.

The DFS pilots had barely any time to prepare, as they had arrived just a few days before the launch of 'Merkur', reassembling their machines and carrying out numerous arduous loading and unloading exercises. It was not until 18-19 May that the glider personnel were informed of their imminent objective. All the gliders were assigned to the Sturmregiment detachments involved in the first wave tasked with capturing the large airfield at Maleme, the large natural harbour of Suda Bay and the Cretan capital, Chania. These three points were fiercely defended by the Greek-British garrison. It would nonetheless still be the first 'mass' glider assault in history. Only ten had landed at Ében-Émael and six at Corinth. But what the Germans could not know was that their arrival was expected...

A rare colour view of DFS 230s at Eleusis. The MG 34 strapped to the side of the cockpit could be fired from the cockpit — note the zip in the fuselage skinning (behind the man bending) enabling a hand to reach out into the slipstream to pull the gun's trigger. Barbed wire is wrapped around the landing skid to help braking. Note the Kapok-filled life jackets on the ground. VIA PAUL STIPDONK

LLG 1 DFS 230 being prepared for the flight to Crete.

Having arrived by rail, DFS 230s were reassembled at Sedes, Salonika's airfield.

Eleusis, Greece, shortly before the launch of 'Merkur'. Note the coloured band around the fuselage, obscuring the Balkenkreuz. This was intended to make it easier to identify the different 'Staffeln' (Schweizer, Richter, Kornemann, etc.).

Fw Hans-Joachim Busse, pilot of one of the five gliders belonging to the Stab flight of 7. Fl. D. recalled what happened during the early hours of 20 May: "The night of 19 to 20 May was short. It proved impossible to sleep with the tension, anticipation and the heat. We were up at 3am. We swallowed a breakfast without much appetite, and left our bags with our personal belongings and our names and addresses. Then it was off to our gliders. We had set up our five machines in a compact formation so that we could hook them onto the tugs as quickly as possible once the other aircraft have taken off."

The arrival of the glider-borne forces was preceded by targeted bomber and Stuka attacks to soften up the target area.

"I flew as the right wingman (rechter Kettenhund) while to the left of Oblt Willy Kruppe (Süssmann's pilot) was Eugen Moser's glider (a veteran of Corinth). The other two aircraft of the Stab flight followed. General Süssmann's Stab waited patiently by the runway. A formation of Stukas took off for Crete. A reddish-yellow dust blanketed the whole airfield for several minutes – which slowed down the take-offs of the other machines. We loaded our gliders. In view of the probable losses, it was decided to divide the staff officers between the five machines."

This proved to be a wise precaution, as was soon realised.

"Behind me is Major Konrad Graf Uxküll-Gyllenband. I wait for everyone to get in. I check that all the equipment stowed between the seats is secure. I close the doors myself and signal that we can't take anything more. The glider is on the verge of being overloaded. I stand fiercely on guard and repel some of the Stab's 'pen-pushers' who are trying to smuggle in more crates of typewriters and office equipment. I glanced at Oblt Kruppe's machine, the cargo area behind the seats is still being filled with packages of all kinds. Finally, Kruppe takes his seat and closes the door. A quick check of the controls. The canopy is closed again. We're ready to go. When the dust has settled a little, our Ju 52s take off. We lift off; even Kruppe's machine – tail-heavy and probably sensitive on the controls – gets airborne. Thank goodness for that!

"We climb slowly because the Ju 52s are also full of parachutists. Over the harbour of Piraeus, we jettison our wheels. We are now heading out across the open sea. I was glad that my machine still responded to the controls. The other 'Kettenhunde' seem to have correctly trimmed their gliders too. Only Oblt Kruppe's machine seemed to be having some trouble. I can see how much pressure he is putting on the control stick as it is thrust hard forward. We climb and alter around

30 minutes we are at 800m and approaching the small island of Aegina. Then three He 111s (probably from KG 26) appeared heading towards us, barely 50m above us. We began to pitch under the 'wash' (turbulence) of their propellers. Kruppe cannot keep his machine level, it pitches hard up and down three times. Suddenly both wings are torn off, the cable snaps and, like a rocket, the fuselage plummets towards the sea. I would later learn that the glider had hit the ground at Aegina. These were the first casualties of Operation Merkur."

Generalleutnant Süssmann – a former Kommodore of KG 55 and commanding 7. Fliegerdivision – was killed in the DFS 230 crash on Aegina. It was very likely that this disaster was due to the aircraft being overloaded. Despite this chilling spectacle, the glider force ploughed on.

"I waggled my wings to report to Moser. I have to say something and attempt to ease the tension. I turn to the Major and say, 'Major, we can see now that it was a good thing to divide up the staff'. My Ju 52 has now taken the lead. We are still climbing. Despite the sun's rays, the horizon is drowned in mist. It's only when you look straight down that you can see the sea and the spray of the waves. We've reached 2,000m. The air is calm but we have to focus all our attention on the Junkers as the horizon is very indistinct. We were flying over a series of islands to the east of the Peloponnese, and then all we could see was the immensity of the sea."

Kommandeur Wenning (KG z.b.V. 105) had departed from Tanagra with his 46 Ju 52s as part of Gruppe West. He was scheduled to drop Major Stentzler's II./Sturm-Rgt west of Maleme. In his report he states that the first Ju 52/DFS 230 Schleppzüge got airborne in complete darkness at 0430: "...slowly, far too slowly, the others followed..." The wheeled-dolly of each of the DFS 230s was being jettisoned perilously close to where other aircraft were waiting to get airborne. And the clouds of dust being kicked up – despite damping operations with water tankers – meant that aircraft taxying and taking-off were barely distinguishable.

Once airborne, flying the heavily-laden Ju 52 transporter demanded a certain level of airmanship: "The flight continued on over the bizarre vegetation-less mountains of the southern Greek peninsula, the Peloponnese. Often the steep rocky ridges were so close under the aircraft that you imagined you could reach out and touch them, and once my pilot, Ofw Nowak, only managed with great difficulty to pull the aircraft – already largely overtaxed – up over a ridge whose real height was underestimated. That didn't seem to be a good omen..."

By now Fw Busse was approaching the coast of Crete: "We had been flying for two hours. Islets appeared again. The Ju 52s then turned west to avoid the powerful anti-aircraft guns deployed on the northern coast of Crete. We are now at an altitude of 2,800m. The island's mountains were emerging from the mist. The tension was growing. The Ju 52s are heading back south. We are about 10km from the island and the flak cannot reach us. We fly a turn to the east. We have reached the coast.

"My Ju 52 waggled its wings. I release the tow cable ('das Ausklinken'), detach myself and the other gliders do the same. The Ju 52s move away. Our four gliders are getting closer. I consult my altimeter. We're not descending. Surprising with a load of over one ton... We must be carried by a strong wind. I can see the Levka mountains, which are 2,000m high. We have to avoid them because we have to land in the Agya depression. I waggle my wings to signal to Moser that we're going to have to dive. I do the same for the other two machines and let out the dive brakes. The nose plunged towards the ground, the speed increased and my altimeter told me that we were losing 10m per second. The indicator reads 200km/h. The sound of the slipstream grew louder. I glanced at the wingtips, but the aircraft had been put together well and we had nothing to worry about. We lost altitude very quickly and speed was our trump card, as we would later discover that only the last of our

20 May 1941. Take-off from Topolia. The Ju 52 engines kick up huge amounts of dust and sand, considerably hampering the task of the glider pilots.

gliders took hits in the vertical plane. Maleme airfield came into view. The first anti-aircraft fire came from behind and below us. Our speed had caught out the enemy…"

On the ground, Christopher Woodhouse, a young officer attached to the staff of General Bernard Freyberg, Commander-in-Chief of the troops defending the island had just brought a message to his superior: "Shortly before dawn on 20 May, I went to see Freyberg at his HQ in Chania. I have absolutely no recollection of the message or why I was there. I remember that he invited me to share his breakfast on the terrace of his villa. The sky was an intense blue – a perfect summer's day. But when I happened to look up, I was astonished to see the sky full of paratroopers and gliders. This did nothing to disturb Freyberg's meal. He contemplated the spectacle, grunted and said: 'Good, they're on time!'"

Indeed, thanks to Ultra, 'Merkur' had been revealed and the detachments of the Cretan garrison had been suitably dispersed over the airborne landing areas. It is probable that the British knew the German plans far better than most of those responsible for carrying them out. Churchill, demanding that Crete be held at all costs, had even insisted that the decrypted messages be sent to the island to be delivered personally to Freyberg – even at the risk of exposing this strictly and fiercely guarded secret.

Feldwebel Busse of LLG 1 put his machine down at dawn: "We were now under a thousand metres. I pushed a little harder on the stick. Our speed reached 240km/h. Shells exploded in the sky and there were detonations everywhere. Our target was the Zuchthaus (or prison. Hence 'Prison Valley', located just south-west of Chania). The building was spotted. We were now quite low over the Agya basin, at a height of 10m, passing over olive trees. Another two kilometres by my reckoning. We saw a large meadow to the left of the prison. We're going to land there. I shout to my passengers: 'Brace, brace! Landing imminent,' and let out the airbrakes. At 100km/h, I was flying over the long grass. The barbed wire around the glider's skid made a swooshing sound as it

Flying to Crete in gliders that were often heavily overloaded.

This DFS 230 has likely hit an obstacle on landing and the bodies of its former occupants lie strewn across the ground.

A glider seen near Maleme. The fuselage band is clearly visible.

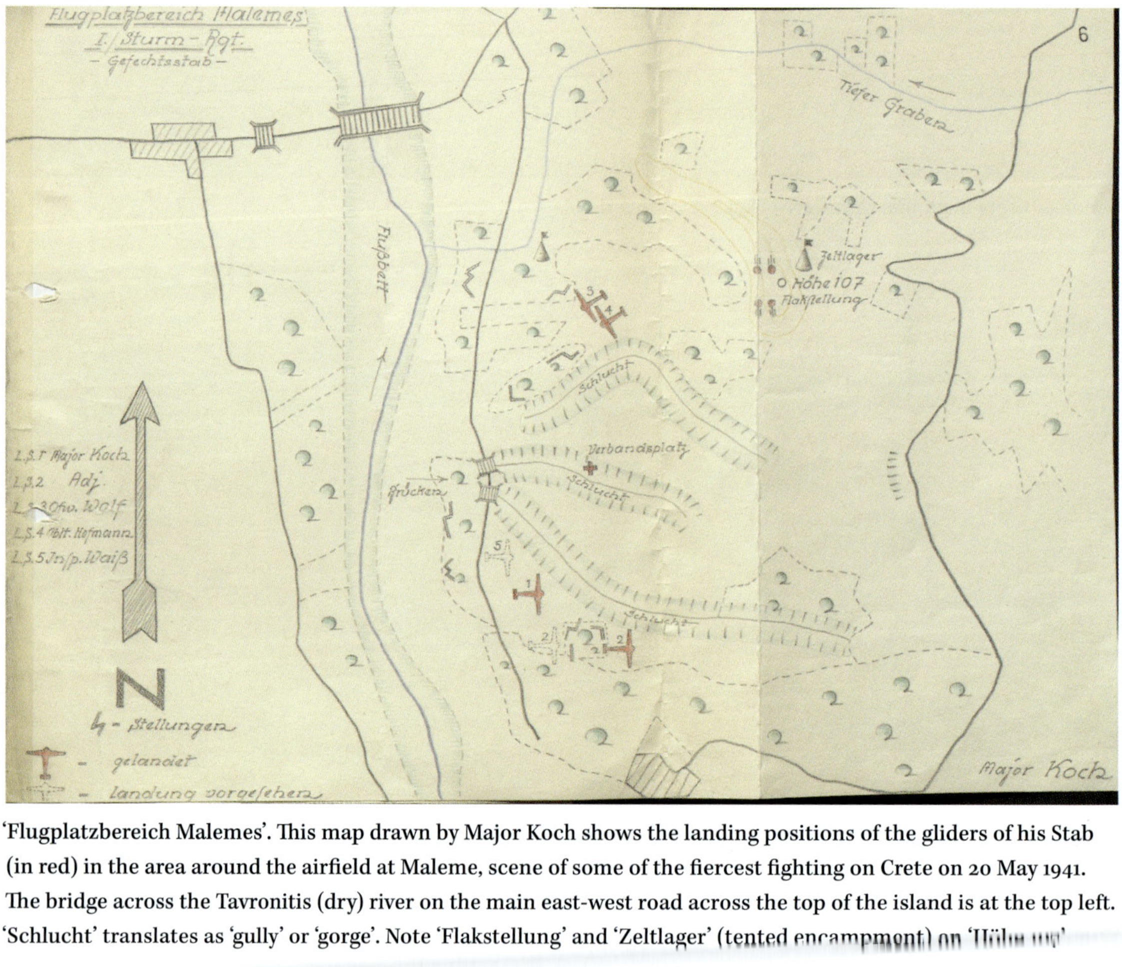

'Flugplatzbereich Malemes'. This map drawn by Major Koch shows the landing positions of the gliders of his Stab (in red) in the area around the airfield at Maleme, scene of some of the fiercest fighting on Crete on 20 May 1941. The bridge across the Tavronitis (dry) river on the main east-west road across the top of the island is at the top left. 'Schlucht' translates as 'gully' or 'gorge'. Note 'Flakstellung' and 'Zeltlager' (tented encampment) on 'Höhe 107'.

A relatively intact DFS 230 on Crete with fuselage band.

slowed us down. We came to a stand after sliding for a hundred metres or so. The other gliders landed close by. All are more or less intact. We have reached our objective. The door is thrown open, along with the canopy. We emerge from the aircraft, guns at the ready and take cover in the tall grass..."

I./Sturmregiment lost three gliders on the way to Crete. After taking off from Eleusis at 0430, one pilot was taken ill while flying over the Aegean Sea. The uncontrollable movements of the glider caused the cable to break. As the stricken DFS 230 pitched nose down, the parachutist seated just behind the pilot kept his cool and, grabbing the stick over the inert body, righted the aircraft (probably thanks to the machine's finesse and excellent handling).

The pilot regained consciousness and managed to ditch the heavily-laden glider in the sea. The men evacuated as quickly as possible before being quickly rescued by a Seenot air-sea rescue aircraft. But without the pilot who, probably exhausted, drowned. The second glider was apparently detached from the Ju 52 for reasons unknown (which was the fate of the occupants). The third DFS 230 (a 3.Kp machine that also suffered a broken cable) managed to land on an islet 30km off Crete.

But what about the fighting itself?

According to author Jean-Paul Pallud, the staff of 7. Fliegerdivision landed near Agya with four gliders. The Chief of Staff, Major i.G. von Uxküll, took command following the disappearance of Süssmann.

Successfully landed by DFS 230 were the Stab and 3. and 4. Kompanien of the Sturmbatallion. In the vanguard of Generalmajor Meindl's regiment, the men of I. Battalion landed in gliders at 0715 to the west and south of Maleme airfield. 3. Kompanie landed as planned at the mouth of the river

Tavronitis and captured an anti-aircraft battery, but Kompaniechef Oblt Wulff Baron von Plessen, was killed by heavy machine-gun fire. 4. Kompanie landed south of the runway on either side of Hill 107, right on top of the positions held by the 22nd Battalion (New Zealand).

Casualties were heavy. The company commander, Oblt Kurt Sarrazin, was also killed, while the battalion commander, Major Walther Koch, and his superior Meindl were seriously wounded. The Kommandeur of the Sturm-Rgt, General Meindl, maintained overall command despite his chest wound but as his condition deteriorated and he drifted in and out of consciousness, the decision was taken to organise his evacuation. LLG 1 pilot Freiherr Egbert von Könitz flew to Maleme the following morning and landed his Ju 52 under fire on the beach and flew Meindl back to

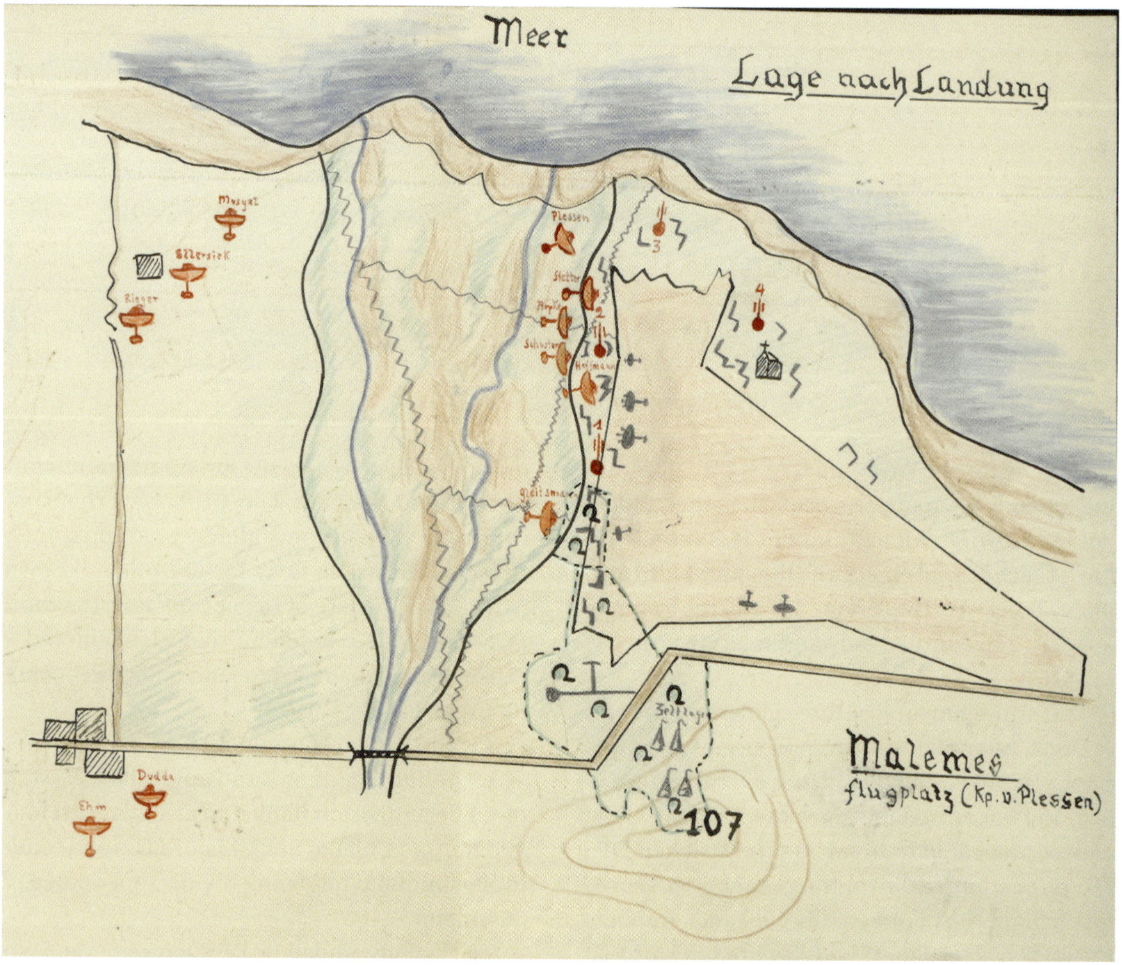

'Lage nach Landung'—extracted from the post-battle 'Gefechtsbericht' report, this 'situation on landing' plan details the landing sites of 3.Kp DFS 230s to the west of the airfield at Maleme and the slopes of Hill 107. Note that von Plessen's DFS 230 is the most northerly of the 3.Kp gliders. The road bridge is at the bottom of the drawing. Landing troops by DFS 230 enabled 'force' to be concentrated against a specified objective important to the overall effort. BAARCH RL33/36

Two views of glider '3' of 3. Kompanie, splintered and split open on the stony ground. Note the lower wing surface skinning ripped open by bullet impacts. Kompaniechef was the 24-year-old Oblt Wulff Baron von Plessen. Von Plessen landed as planned at the mouth of the (dry) Tavronitis river. Leading his men south towards the bridge he was killed by heavy machine gun fire as he approached the olive groves. VIA STIPDONK/MEYER

Athens. Von Könitz was later a Kp.Fü in Fallschirm-Aufklärungs-Abt.12. He was killed in Normandy; according to one eyewitness his body was found hanging from a telegraph pole in St Lambert sur Dive (Falaise Gap) on 18-19 August 1944.

Of the 29 gliders that took off from Eleusis, one was lost at sea, while another (belonging to the battalion staff flight) made a very hard landing and hit an obstacle, killing or seriously injuring its occupants. As Georg Schlauch wrote, "Clouds of dust made visibility on the island very poor. The gliders had to put down somewhere – but they could not see where they were. Five 4. Kompanie DFS 230s completely missed the designated landing area and, touching down on very stony and rutted terrain, some were wrecked with fatal consequences for the squads on board. One of the two Art.Rgt. gliders carrying two heavy guns crashed, probably killing its occupants. Four gliders from 3. Company (reduced to 11 DFS 230s) separated too late from their tugs and arrived at the target at too high a speed. Crashes occurred and several airborne personnel were injured. The other seven gliders landed safely."

The nine Stosstrupp Braun gliders landed near the Tavronitis bridge (spanning the dry riverbed cutting through the east-west coast road to the west of Maleme) and the men launched an assault under a deluge of fire. One DFS 230 landed very close to the bridge, enabling its occupants to defuse the charges attached to the bridge's supports. The bridge was taken, but casualties were heavy and Major Franz Braun was killed. The other battalions of the Sturmregiment then parachuted to the east and west of Maleme.

Kampfgruppe Altmann – comprising the 1.

Major Franz Braun and several of his men were quickly killed in the fighting for the Tavronitis bridge. They were hurriedly buried in a mass grave 'decorated' with a DFS 230 canopy section.

and 2. Kompanien of the Luftlande Sturmregiment – was to land in gliders to seize important points near Chania while parachutists from FJR 3 jumped to the south-east of the town. The Kampfgruppe was not as successful as expected however. The second company (plus one section) under the command of Hptm Gustav Altmann himself landed with its 15 gliders on the Akrotiri peninsula. Some of the batteries that were supposed to be captured turned out to be decoys and the adventure soon turned into a disaster as the sector was held in force by the Northumberland Hussars. Of the 136 airborne troops that landed, 108 were soon lost. Hptm Altmann was captured with two of his section leaders. The third was killed. The 1. Kpie (minus one section) under the command of Oblt Alfred Genz landed with nine gliders south-east of Chania and captured anti-aircraft batteries as planned. As it seemed impossible to make contact with the rest of the unit, Genz withdrew southwards.

A pilot in the group led by Oblt Genz, Ogfr W Kolleger (St Nüse/LLG 1), had a narrow escape: "We boarded our glider at 0414. I was in glider No. 2 to the left of the Kette. The ground crew 'Starthelfer' greeted me, wishing me good luck. As I closed my canopy, I heard one of them exclaim: "Thank God I'm not flying in one of those!" Take-off was at 0430. As I left the ground, it became clear that my glider was handicapped by the presence of a very heavy mortar. I was finding it increasingly difficult to keep my overloaded aircraft upright. Nevertheless, I somehow managed to get to within about 30km of Crete. When my tug slowed down, I felt the aircraft slipping away from me. At that moment, two Bf 110s flew past at close range and the turbulent 'wash' of their engines rocked my machine."

His tow cable snapped but Kolleger, keeping his cool, headed directly towards his objective, coming from the north and not from the south like the other gliders. At 0650 he put down in one piece near a battery of anti-aircraft guns on the outskirts of Chania. His passengers disembarked and stormed the battery. Twenty minutes later, the six gliders carrying Genz's unit landed nearby. The airborne troops took control of the area but, surrounded, tried in vain to contact Altmann's group. Finally, the next morning, they made a breakthrough during which one of the pilots, Uffz Günther Schulze, was killed with a headshot.

After ten days of fierce and bloody fighting, the island of Crete fell. Reinforcements of paratroopers and Gebirgsjäger and poor or a lack of decision-making by Allied commander Freyberg, which led to the commander on the ground withdrawing from Hill 107, resulted in this surprising success. 'Merkur' should have ended in disaster for the Germans within the first two days. The German victory was essentially due to the adaptability and responsiveness of the airborne troops who, despite being caught in a trap, were able to put up a front and then fight back effectively despite suffering appalling losses.

Forced to abandon the airborne positions in the east and centre of the island to their fate, the 'Merkur' commanders concentrated their efforts from the second day of the landings on the Maleme/Chania sector. The Greek-British defence was crushed there, enabling the pocket to be enlarged and the rest of the island to be gradually conquered. However, it was a 'hollow' victory. The 'butcher's bill' for the Germans was incredibly high – nearly 4,000 elite troops KIA with another 2,000 wounded. It was virtually the end of the Fallschirmjäger as a strategic asset, while Crete itself became very much a 'strategic backwater'.

'Merkur' was a disaster for the glider pilots. The sudden death of Generalleutnant Süssmann and part of his staff was a very bad portent. Shortly afterwards, at least three gliders came down in the sea. But these were relatively limited losses given the arduous two-hour flight over water with overloaded gliders, towed by heavily loaded transports. On landing, the airborne troops faced a reception committee. Although some gliders were badly

A burnt-out DFS 230 in the dry bed of the Tavronitis. Note the grave, topped with a Fallschirmjäger helmet, possibly the pilot's.

A Fallschirmer in typical 'Knochensack' jump smock seen on Maleme airfield.

Gliders scattered near the bridge.

damaged when they hit ('landed on') the hard and uneven stony ground, crew losses were minimal compared with those of the paratroopers.

Contrary to what would later be written, relatively few Fallschirmjäger were killed during their descent. It was only after they had touched down and as they discarded their parachutes and ran to the weapons containers to grab their weapons that they were 'shot like rabbits'. The speed of the gliders as they launched into their 'dives' caught out the anti-aircraft defences and, as soon as they landed, their occupants emerged, weapons in hand, immediately operational. It was therefore unfortunate for the German airborne arm that it did not have more than 70 DFS 230s available for Crete. Had more been deployed, their losses may have been less severe.

As they came down on the island (thanks to information provided by Ultra), the platoons arriving in gliders were immediately in contact with the enemy. As every man was useful, the pilots did not remain in the background as on previous missions. Of the 69 pilots involved in 'Merkur', 23 were killed and one captured. Another 15 or so were wounded.

The use of gliders during the Crete campaign was to have a very different impact on the two sides of the Channel. Stunned by the fall of the heavily defended island, the London government searched high and low for an explanation before finding it in the use of gliders, a devastating weapon that had brought down the impregnable Belgian fortress of Ében-Émael. British newspapers described a sky full of DFS 230s and, for the occasion, even invented the story of 'trains' of up to three gliders towed by a single Ju 52, even though the overloaded trimotor transports were hard pushed to tow even a single glider when fully laden. For their part, German propaganda services deliberately kept silent about the actions of the DFS 230. In the Germans' own account of 'Merkur' entitled 'Kreta, Sieg der Kühnsten' ('Crete, victory of the most daring') published in 1942, which brought together hundreds of photos of the fighting on the island (the work of Bildberichter correspondents on the ground), there are no images of gliders. In his after-action report (BA RL 33/116), Student wrote: "Flying in an unprotected, slow-moving, cumbersome aircraft at heights of between 100m and 200m in heavy defensive fire is highly demanding for all crews. Any necessary changes of heading at low altitude in strange terrain with no possibility of curving away and flying another approach represent under these circumstances the most difficult task that can be asked of a crew."

He was referring to the Kampgruppen z.b.V. He could just as equally have been referring to the challenges faced by the DFS 230 pilots.

OPERATION MERCURY LOSSES

Almost exactly one year after their successes in Belgium, the Luftwaffe's DFS 230 assault gliders were back in action, but enjoyed mixed fortunes. The Corinth operation had got off to a very good start, with the gliders landing their assault troops in record time very close to the bridge and surprising the defenders, as had been the case at Ében-Émael. As luck would have it, the bridge was blown and, despite this relative failure, a Ritterkreuz was awarded to honour the airborne personnel who carried out this daring mission.

According to figures compiled by Georg Schlaug, the glider losses during Operation 'Mercury' were as follows:

* **Stab 7. Fliegerdivision:** one aircraft crashed at Aegina.
* **Stab, 3. and 4. Kpie of the Sturmbataillion:** probably two gliders fell into the sea and a third landed on an islet. Another is believed to have crashed on landing.
* **Stosstrupp Braun:** two or three DFS 230s 'crashed' (one at sea?).
* **Art.Rgt:** one aircraft 'crashed'.
* **Kampfgruppe Altmann:** no losses.

Of the 69 gliders that took off from the mainland, it can therefore be estimated that at least half a dozen failed to reach Crete. On landing, around ten others were destroyed (due to excessive speed or obstacles on the ground). According to the official list of losses, 37 DFS 230s were abandoned or lost in Greece/Crete. This figure could be increased to 45.

The losses are listed under various Staffel 'names' (sub-sections of LLG 1?), the origins of which are unknown: 'Staffel Schweizer', 'Staffel Richter', etc. (possible code names, or the designation of the airmen's initial unit).

Whatever the case, these were the casualties:

* **Staffel Schweizer. Killed:** Ogfr Karl Meier and Uffz Hans-Karsten Schoening. **Wounded:** Oblt Josef Karl, Gefr Helmut Berthauer, Fw Fritz Haupt, Gefr Kurt Hupka, Uffz Fritz Prüssner and Fw Walter.
* **Staffel Richter. Killed:** Gefr Hermann Bülle, Uffz Heinrich Hack, Uffz Helmut Hauck, Oblt Herbert Kaiser, Uffz Werner Kerkmann, Uffz Friedrich Nagel, Uffz Helmut Schupp and Uffz Alexander Ullrich. **Injured:** Ogfr Fritz Horn, Gefr Wilhelm Köhler, Lt Ruppert (Rupprecht?) Pongratz and Gefr Heinz Weidemann. **PG:** Fw Heinrich Bösebeck.

Based on the names, it seems that the 'Staffel Richter' was attached to the Gruppe Altmann.

* **Staffel Nüse. Killed:** Gefr Rolf Baasch, Gefr Heinrich Binneger, Uffz Günther Brinkmann, Oblt Werner Kellner, Uffz Georg Klimke and Uffz Günther Schulze. **Injured:** Gefr Herbert Adomeit.

Based on the names, 'Staffel Nüse' had to be attached to the 1./Sturm Rgt of Oblt Genz.

* **Staffel Graf. Killed:** Fw Helmut Hömke and Fw Max Hübner. **Wounded:** Lt Karl-Heinz Lange.
* **Staffel Konermann. Killed:** Uffz Horst Everth, Gefr Hans Negle, Uffz Otto Schäuffele and Uffz Johannes Steffens. **Wounded:** Uffz Günther Czuday.
* **Stab 7 Fl D. Killed:** Oblt Willi Kruppe.

The loss in action of Uffz Wolfgang Bade and Ogfr Gerhard Gross and the capture of a Lt Henke are sometimes cited. However, these three airmen are said to have been crew members of Ju 52s from LLG 1 shot down in Crete.

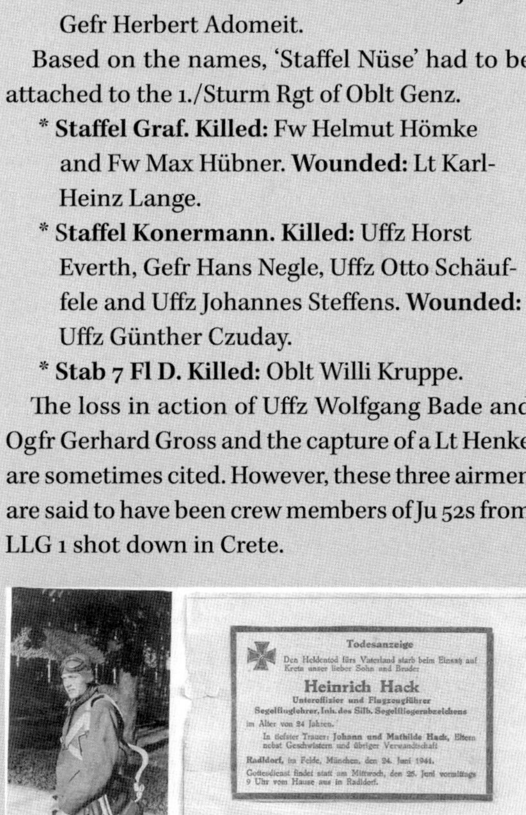

Deathcard notice for Segelflieger (pilot and instructor) Uffz Heinrich Hack of Staffel Richter.

5

THE DFS 230 IN ACTION ON THE EASTERN FRONT

It is often said that General Kurt Student had declared after 'Merkur' that Crete was the 'tomb of the German paratrooper'. Losses had been heavy – for example, of the 503 operational Ju 52s assembled for Crete, nearly 300 had either been destroyed or heavily damaged. With the invasion of the USSR, the Fallschirmjäger went into action mainly as elite infantrymen. The fact is there was no role for the DFS 230 at the start of Barbarossa. Nevertheless, 7. Fliegerdivision kept a few gliders to train its men and transport equipment.

However, if there were no gliders on the Eastern Front in late June 1941, the situation had already changed by late August as the Lastensegler returned mainly to their original function: that of transporters. This was necessary as a result of the huge distances covered by the invading army, the poor quality roads and resupply routes and the far-flung nature of the various fronts.

Preparations for Barbarossa – launched on 22 June 1941 – included the formation of glider transport units. The Luftwaffe was able to field some 280 DFS 230s as well as some 23 of the new Me 321s (although the latter were committed prematurely!).

In May, the glider pilots of 2./LLG 1 started their conversion at Hildesheim on the brand new Gotha Go 242, while 6./LLG 1 sent 25 pilots and 15 DFS 230s to one of the three airfields in Bucharest (Baneasa?) to form a unit under the command of Oblt Paul Hundenborn. Shortly after the reunion of its elements, the unit moved to the airfield under construction at Targsorul Nou (near Ploesti). As soon as the German troops entered the USSR, the DFS 230s, towed by Ju 52s, were to transport supplies to the newly captured airfields. The unit would follow closely the advance of the ground forces and would thus shift to Tiraspol then Nikolajev.

The LS-Kommando Hundenborn was assigned to KG z.b.V. 104 and its primary mission, as the Heer advanced, was to evacuate and repatriate the wounded, while bringing in supplies. Flights were mostly carried out at low altitude for security reasons, which proved to be judicious when, on 28 September, north of Odessa, a formation of gliders was surprised in the air by Soviet fighters. At least three DFS 230s had to urgently separate from their tugs and, thanks to their low altitude, were able to land without difficulty. The pilots (Bader, Neuhaus and Adomeit) were able to evacuate their machines in time before they were 'strafed' by the enemy. Loaded with bombs and fuel, the

The LS-Kdo Hundenborn, a non-offensive supply unit, adopted a very martial badge: an eagle holding a hand grenade in its talons. Note the yellow fuselage stripe.

Kommando Hundenborn regularly supplied JG 52 and JG 77. A member of the latter Geschwader photographed one of this detachment's gliders at Sarabus.

Close-up of the LS-Kommando badge.

A DFS 230 towed by an Hs 126 (probably from the detachment based at Vitebsk) brought in drums of fuel.

DFS 230 at Nikolajev-Ost, on 3 March 1943. In the cockpit is Kucharzik. Standing from left are Kruse, Haake and Peters. VIA PAUL STIPDONK

DFSs were destroyed.

A fourth glider was damaged but its pilot, the unit commander (Paul Hundenborn), was only slightly injured. Herbert Adomeit, who narrowly escaped death, was one of the few DFS 230 pilots wounded in Crete on 20 May 1941 who had quickly returned to a frontline unit. At the end of 1941, with bad weather beginning to hit and both ground and air units pinned down, Kommando Hundenborn was sent back to the Reich.

Another DFS 230 unit was to operate from Poland. In July 1941, 18 DFS 230 gliders of III./LLG 1 reached Mielec from Goslar. Under the orders of Lt Neumann, this detachment (assigned to KG z.b.V 1) moved to Proskurov (Ukraine) to supply the Wehrmacht units dispersed around Krivoy Rog, Vinnitsa and Zhitomir. These flights lasted only three months because LS-Kdo Neumann was disbanded in October and returned to Goslar.

To supply the central sector of the new Eastern Front, a detachment of DFS 230s towed by Hs 126s left Parchim and settled for a short time in Borissov before moving to Vitebsk. With its own tugs, this autonomous unit (LS-Staffel 230) was not subordinated to a Ju 52 squadron. Back to Parchim in September, the detachment left shortly after for the USSR, operating from Novgorod and Konotop. The return to Parchim was definitive in October 1941.

At least one offensive operation was flown in the East in 1941 by the DFS 230: Operation Beowulf, took place over the Baltic and comprised landings on the Estonian island of Saaremaa (Ösel in German and Swedish) where the Soviet army had established a complex of artillery batteries capable of hindering both the German advance on land and interfering with maritime traffic along the Baltic coasts. These had to be eliminated but the island's difficult terrain (coupled with the enemy's defences) limited the possibilities. The German High Command therefore decided to repeat the actions of Ében-Émael and Corinth.

This time the attackers were not Fallschirmjäger but members of the Brandenbürger (referred to after the war as 'the commandos of the Reich'). The 16th volunteer company, based in Düren awaiting action, was designated to operate as an airborne unit at Ösel under the orders of Hptm Benesch. While the Brandenbürgers were heading east, 6./LLG 1 sent ten gliders (with tugs) to Seerappen (East Prussia) from Halberstadt on July 5. The Schleppzüge made several stops before the detachment reached Pernau (Estonia) on September 13. The airmen were briefed on their mission while meeting the 'commandos'. The next day, five gliders loaded with soldiers took off in the early morning. This detachment was placed under the orders of Uffz Alexander Haag and four pilots are designated for the mission: Thielmann, Rössler, Kommander and Hertwig. To silence the anti-aircraft batteries, the small formation was supported by Bf 110s from II./ZG 76.

According to Hptm Benesch, head of the commando: "During our meeting, the general in charge of the mission told me of the plan. The assault on the island of Ösel was to be carried out by sappers transported in assault boats ... But what could the Brandenbürgers do? The study of maps and aerial photos revealed a clear space near the battery. As the water was very low in this area and the area was marshy, sending ships was not recommended but gliders could be used ... These would be escorted by a Gruppe of Messerschmitt Bf 110s. On September 14, 1941, 50 men took off from the makeshift strip at Pernau at night in five DFS 230s towed by Ju 52s. The very risky nocturnal departure took place without incident.

"During the flight, dawn broke, revealing the outline of the peninsula. The order was given to the pilots to land, which was done immediately. The cable was released and the first glider sped towards its objective in an accelerated dive, in compact formation with the other four aircraft. At this point, the Bf 110s proved very useful by strafing everything that moved on the ground (Note: the Kommandeur of the Bf 110 unit is described as 'the Hptm von R'; apparently Ralph von Rettberg leading II./ZG 26).

"The pilot shouted to us that we were going to land 'too short' and we hit the ground in front of the fortification bunkers. We rushed out to try to penetrate the defensive circle but the positions were already occupied by the Soviets who fired at us with machine guns. We had to take cover, the surprise effect of our attack having now faded. We now had to coordinate our efforts with the group that had landed by sea but we saw no trace of them. We then chose to form a bridgehead while waiting for the arrival of maritime reinforcements.

"Subjected to continuous fire from the Bf 110s, the bunkers caused us less trouble but the adversary committed its reserves behind our backs. These soldiers arrived by trucks nearby and almost hand-to-hand fighting began. Time passed and we still saw nothing coming, the 110 remaining our only supports. The Soviets stopped their assaults but, as evening fell, fear grew as our air support would disappear. In the evening, the Ju 52s which had towed us flew over us and dropped rubber boats, most of which fell on enemy territory. However, we were able to recover five of them to reach the east coast."

With the energy of despair, those still able paddled back to the mainland. Only 31 of them returned and two pilots were killed including Uffz Alexander Haag and Flg Karl Kommander.

Following the failure of this operation, the 61. Infanteriedivision was committed with the support of the four Me 321 gliders of GS 1. On September 21, the crew Noske/Seidel whose Gigant was towed by three Bf 110s, brought in 20,000 litres of fuel and four tons of ammunition. The next day, Winkler's crew did the same. These four Giganten were written off but following its chaotic start Operation Beowulf ended with success, the Germans completely reoccupying the island on October 21, 1941. 6./LLG 1 left the Baltic to return to Halberstadt.

IN-DEPTH REORGANISATION

In an effort to standardise the glider force, the Luftwaffe High Command ordered Student's glider and transport command XI. Fliegerkorps to reorganise the glider units. The result was the establishment of ten DFS 230 Staffeln (each comprising 15 gliders and two He 46s) and six Go 242 Staffeln (15 gliders with He 111 tugs).

Manpower was to be provided by LLG 1, Erg. Gr. (S) 1 from Langendiebach, Erg. Gr. (S) 2 from Posen and the remnants of the Go 242 units engaged in the East.

The three Gruppen of LLG 1 were 'downsized' and transformed into Übungsgruppe with smaller numbers. This made it possible to 'divert' 22 Ju 52s from I./LLG 1 which, under the name of 'Einsatzgruppe I./LLG 1', were sent to the Mediterranean to reinforce the Afrika Korps supply fleet. The 'dismantling' of the Geschwader was significant, as III./LLG 1 was reduced to just a single 9. Staffel, with the rest of the personnel and equipment being distributed to the other units flying the DFS 230.

Four liaison staffs, VK(S) (Verbindungskommando Schlepper) responsible for coordinating glider actions in the east, were created with LLG 1 personnel:

* **VK(S) 1:** attached to Luftflotte 1 with Oberst Otto Brandes, previously Kommandeur of Stukavorschule 1, as Kommandeur.
* **VK (S) 2:** attached to Luftflotte 2 with Hptm Herbert Fromert as Kommandeur.
* **VK (S) 4:** attached to Luftflotte 4. Kommandeur: Hptm Joseph Schossig.
* **VK (S) V:** attached to the Lw.Kdo. Ost. Kommandeur: Obstlt Friedrich Edler von Braun.

The new Staffeln of DFS 230 were designated by numbers from 1 to 10; those of the Go 242 from 1 to 6. While this appears to have been a straightforward numbering system, each command soon assigned the units new and rather convoluted names. These 'independent' Staffeln were assigned to the Eastern Front and to the Mediterranean primarily to carry out transport duties.

Glider Staffel	New designation	Assigned to
1. DFS 230 Staffel	1. (DFS)/VIII	VIII. Fliegerkorps
4. DFS 230 Staffel	1. (DFS)/Lw.Kdo.Don	Lw.Kdo.Don
5. DFS 230 Staffel	1. (DFS)/VK (S) 4	Luftflotte 4
6. DFS 230 Staffel	1. (DFS)/VK (S) 1	Luftflotte 1
7. DFS 230 Staffel	1. (DFS)/VK (S) V	Lw.Kdo. Don
8. DFS 230 Staffel	1. (DFS)/VK (S) 2	Luftflotte 2
9. DFS 230 Staffel	2. (DFS)/VK (S) 2	Luftflotte 2

Note 2. and 3. DFS 230 Staffeln were disbanded in July 1942. The multiple changes of unit designation were not only confusing but indicated a lack of preparation on the part of the higher command with regard to the role that gliders were to play and their distribution by theatres of war. Meanwhile, as units were being formed and disbanded (sometimes very quickly), training of glider pilots continued in the Reich.

Training school discussion in front of a DFS 230. This is a C-variant which featured the additional loading door ahead of the wing on the port side.

At Zellhausen, a pilot 'harnesses up' before take-off

Two views of a DFS 230 and its tug, a parasol-winged Heinkel He 46. Note the swastika painted on the glider's tailplane, rarely displayed on these machines.

6

SPECIAL 'OPS' IN NORTH AFRICA

DFS 230 gliders were also deployed in North Africa in support of Rommel's Deutsche Afrikakorps or DAK. His overly ambitious offensive towards Egypt in mid-1941 – well beyond the scope of the missions assigned to his corps – came up against British led counteroffensives with varying results ('Battleaxe' and 'Crusader'). The war in the African desert was literally nothing more than a series of advances and retreats.

The retreat of the Axis forces was attributable to the lengthening of the lines of communication, resulting in a scarcity of supplies. The British had the advantage of having a rear base, Egypt, while the Axis forces had to depend largely on irregular supplies from Europe. German shipping was regularly sunk by the Royal Navy while aerial resupply missions flown by Ju 52s were thoroughly harassed by the RAF. The new Gotha Go 242 gliders were far more suitable for these sorts of missions. December 1941 was a disastrous time for the German glider forces, as the Go 242s in Africa were overwhelmed by the British offensive. During 1942 the desert conflict had become a supply war. Fortress Tobruk finally fell on 21 June 1942 and the Afrika Korps now had to push on towards Cairo. The Ju 52s of LLG 1 were withdrawn from their unit to bring food and ammunition to Feldmarschall Erwin Rommel's troops, as well as evacuating the wounded.

Not all the Lastensegler present in Libya in 1942 belonged to transport units. Some DFS 230s were in fact assigned to Ju 87 Gruppen, and one version of the Stuka (the D-2) was equipped with a tow-rope attachment. These gliders made it easier to move equipment from airfield to airfield and brought in fuel supplies when the aircraft were based far from built-up areas or the only coastal road, the famous Via Balbia.

The bulk of the gliders had arrived around June/July 1942: two Staffeln of DFS 230s and two more of Go 242s under Verbindungskommando (S) 2.

The first Staffel to head south was 1 (DFS)/VK (S) 2 under Oblt Schumacher. Reassembled at Lecce airfield, the DFS 230s were towed by Ju 52s to Tobruk, via Kalamaki (the airfield near Athens) and Maleme (on the island of Crete). Henschel Hs 126s were to follow, as the Ju 52s were overloaded and could no longer be used to tow simple gliders.

1 (DFS)/VK (S) 2 arrived piecemeal, but its first elements were immediately committed to supplying Tobruk to Fuka, transporting food, fuel and ammunition. The pilots soon discovered the pitfalls of the desert, such as sandstorms, snakes and scorpions, and the sometimes rocky, sometimes very rough terrain – in short, a headache during take-offs and landings. Not to mention the

A DFS 230 of the 1. (DFS)/VK (S) 2 in Africa. Note the unit's 'African' badge.

malaria that could affect all personnel...

IThe second DFS 230 Staffel, 2 (DFS)/VK (S) 2, led by Oblt Erich Hartig, was reconstituted far too late at Lecce, in September, after its descent to the south. With the British having launched their offensive at El Alamein, the transfer of the unit to the other side of the Mediterranean was limited. The DFS pilots were rushed into the two Go 242 Staffeln and had to familiarise themselves with this heavier glider as quickly as possible. It should be noted that the 2. (DFS)/VK (S) 2 had only old He 46s as tugs... aircraft totally unsuited to the conditions at the time.

Oblt Hoff's 2. (Go)/VK (S) 2 arrived at Lecce in June 1942, but soon lost two Gothas that fell into the sea after a cable broke during the transfer flight to Greece. It seems that at least five Go 242s were destroyed in this way, but each time the crew was rescued by the Seenot (air-sea rescue). The Go 242s were much appreciated by the troops because, unlike the Ju 52s and DFS 230s already present in Africa, they could carry guns or light vehicles in their holds.

The 1 (Go)/VK (S) 2 arrived in the Mediterranean at Athens-Kalamaki, while the 2 (Go)/VK (S) 2 remained at Lecce. From the bottom of the Italian boot, the Go 242s, now towed by He 111s from KG 4, made five-hour flights over the sea. According to Uffz Kutzas, one of the DFS 230 pilots assigned to the Gotha: "As the Gotha Staffel needed pilots, I was second pilot on a mission to Africa. Up to that point, I had only ever flown the DFS 230. We took off from Lecce for Tobruk. We were carrying 15 drums of fuel and several others of oil. Our flight lasted four and a half hours at around 3-5m above the surface of the sea. It was

A Ju 87 (probably from StG 3) has towed this DFS 230 to its makeshift airfield established in the Libyan desert.

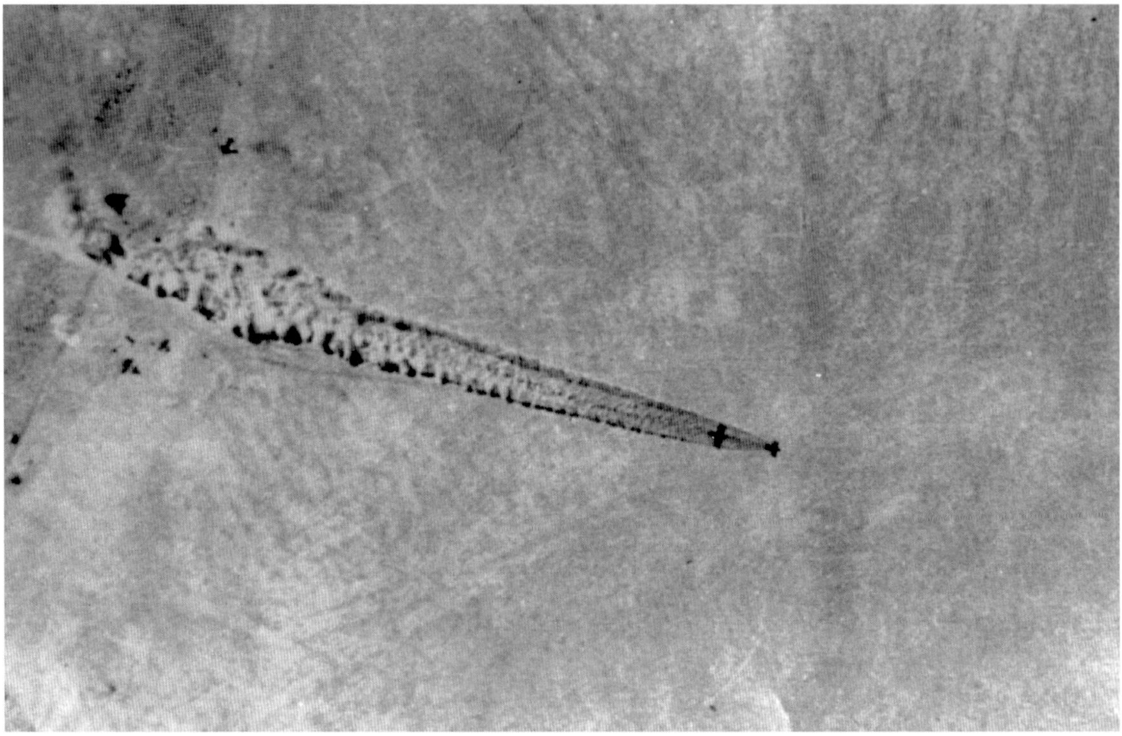

A British reconnaissance aircraft photographed the takeoff of a Ju 87 towing a DFS 230 while raising clouds of sand.

particularly hard on the pilot, who had to hold a heavily loaded glider – over four tons – in his hands. Following a navigational error, we landed at Derna. The next day, we flew to Tobruk and, after unloading, stopped off at Heraklion in Crete because we couldn't refuel in Africa. We then returned to Lecce. It is easy to understand why cables could snap during such flights."

The British offensive that began on 23 October 1942 forced the Axis Panzerarmee Afrika to retreat. Nevertheless, glider crews continued to supply the strong points – including the fortress of Tobruk – right to the end. On 12 November, Oblt Ziegler landed his Gotha at the highly threatened Derna airfield, unloaded drums of fuel and then returned to Kalamaki with no fewer than 28 wounded on board – a considerable number.

Faced with the enemy advance, the personnel of 1. (DFS)/VK (S) 2 evacuated Derna back to Italy in a Ju 90. Six DFS 230s, four Hs 126s and four Ju 87s were scuttled at El Quasaba, Bomba and Tobruk. The official list of losses also indicates the scuttling of a Go 242 but almost certainly the Allies found many other gliders on airfields that the Germans did not have time to repair.

As resupply missions could no longer take place, 1. (Go)/VK (S) 2 left Kalamaki to establish itself in Italy at San Pancrazio near Piacenza (Piacenza) whose airfield houses a school for crews of Ju 87 (towing exercises by Stuka had to take place there). On December 20, Hptm Fromert, leading VK (S) 2, was reported injured in San Pancrazio in the crash of a DFS 230.

Officially, the loss lists mentions around 30 DFS 230s and around 20 Go 242s destroyed in these missions in the Mediterranean but the figures were undoubtedly higher. Although the vast majority of gliders had evacuated Africa, some DFS 230s continued to operate briefly in this theatre of operations on special missions.

SONDERKOMMANDO DORA

Throughout the African campaign, the German high command feared an attack that could come from the south, from the French possessions of Chad. On January 24, 1942, an isolated He 111 took off from the oasis of Hon (500km southeast of Tripoli) to carry out a 'symbolic' attack on Fort Lamy (current Njamena) probably with the aim of testing enemy reactions as well as the possibilities of Luftwaffe bombers over such a long distance.

Fearing incursions by Free French forces, a 'special detachment Dora' was formed from specialists (geographers, geologists, etc.) with vehicles and a few aircraft (including DFS 230s and Go 242s). This detachment, placed under the command of Obstlt Seubert, was based at the oasis of Hon and had a section of Brandenbürger for its protection.

Before and after the start of the British offensive, a pilot attached to this special commando, Fw Parlitz (member of 9./LLG 1), travelled very long distances over the desert, sometimes in the Go 242, sometimes at the controls of a DFS 230, being towed by a He 111 with the task of supplying various oases (Bir Musciuru, Afafi, El Gatrun etc.), headquarters of the various Sonderkommando detachments. And while he encroached on Free French airspace he did not encounter enemy aircraft.

On December 26, 1942, the majority of gliders present at Hon were destroyed in an air attack. The surviving Lastensegler were set on fire or scuttled.

IN TUNISIA

Forced to retreat following the Allied landings in Algeria and Morocco, Panzerarmee Afrika had fallen back to what can be described as 'the Tunisian bridgehead'. To try to alleviate the pressure of this encirclement, it was decided to launch raids on the Algiers-Constantine-Souk el Arba railway line as well as on Constantine-Mekiesna-Tebessa rail route with the bridges as priority objectives.

On December 20, Feldmarschall Albert Kesselring, Oberbefehlshaber Süd, met Hptm Gerhard Schacht at his HQ in Frascati. A paratrooper officer, the latter had led the Gruppe Beton on the Albert Canal and, for this feat of arms, was awarded the Ritterkreuz. He was since attached to the well-known Fallschirmbrigade Ramcke sent shortly before to Libya to support the troops of Feldmarschall Rommel then pushing towards Egypt.

Schacht was assigned six Ju 52s from IV./KG z.b.V. 1 with crews competent on instruments, 12 DFS 230s from 2. (DFS)/VK (S) 2 still present in Lecce as well as three He 111s. On December 26, 1942, from Castelvetrano, the small detachment reached Bizerte. There it was learnt that the mission would take place the next day with the support of the Brandenbürger (the detachment of Hptm Friedrich von Koenen) similarly to the disastrous Ösel operation the previous year. Given the importance of the mission, the briefing took place in the presence of General Martin Harlinghausen, the 'Fliegerführer Tunis'.

The force was divided into two groups:

* Three DFS 230s with pilots Heinzel, Hustert and Bartels to drop the Brandenbürger and von Koenen about 60km north-northwest of Gafsa, i.e. at Sidi Bou Baker.
* Three other DFS 230s were to undertake a similar operation near a bridge north-east of Kasserine. One of the pilots was Oblt Erich Hartig, Staffelkapitän of 2. (DFS)/VK (S) 2. With him, Uffz Fissenewert and another pilot whose name is not known.

A Brandenburg officer, Willi Clormann, left an account of this expedition launched on the evening of December 27: "We flew with ten men in each glider. The pilot was an Oberleutnant of the Luftwaffe who was on the staff of the Fliegerführer in Tunis. (Staffelkapitän Hartig). The leader of the sappers was a certain Lt 'Poldi' Hagenauer. We were supposed to have three gliders but one had to turn back."

According to G. Schlaug, Uffz Fissenewert did not return to Bizerte but was forced to land in the countryside probably following a cable break. This small group was picked up by an aircraft the next day. Clormann's account continues: "We had to land near the railway bridge and blow it up. The Luftwaffe had attempted to bomb it with Stukas on several occasions with no result. We were caught near the objective by anti-aircraft fire and the pilot put down in another valley. Whether as a result of damage or of pilot error, the glider hit the ground very hard and suddenly. The pilot had both legs broken in the crash. He had to be left there with the glider. He was found later by some natives and then handed over to the British..."

Strangely enough, this capture appears officially in the casualty list dated 30 December and not 26 December, while only one glider is mentioned in the report, although at least five were lost. All that remained was for the Germans to try to get back into their lines. Clormann continued: "I led the march, although we had great difficulty supporting the wounded. I had a map. We marched at night and rested during the day. We were also able to find a camel that served as a pack animal and supported our equipment and a wounded man."

During this march, the small troop repelled an attack by French soldiers. They reached their lines six days later, probably with the help of Arab fighters, de facto allies of the Germans. However, nothing is known about the fate of the group in the third glider.

Von Koenen's group also lost one glider. On board Uffz Heinzel's glider was the group led by the man in charge of the operation, Hptm von Koenen. After overflying Cap Bon, the formation flew over the sea then towards Sousse and Sfax before turning west over the Gulf of Gabès. At this point, Ju 88s passed over the Ju 52s and one of the crews recklessly followed them. The three-engined aircraft had to land out of fuel north of Sfax, while Uffz Hustert put his glider down without difficulty.

For their part, the two DFS 230s arrived close to the bridge that would have been blown up despite the lack of a third of their manpower. Then, guided by locals, the 22 men reached the Italian position at Maknassi.

Although the documents contradict each other given the confusion at the time, another operation of this type is said to have taken place on the night of 29/30 December according to two British interrogation reports:

* **Place and date:** Near St Arnaud (Algeria) 30 December 1942. 0300.
* **Type and markings:** DFS 230 glider coded S7+WP.
* **Unit:** Autonomous under Luftwaffe command at Tunis.
* **Pilot:** 5./StG 3.
* **Mission:** took off at 2330 from Bizerte/Sidi Ahmed on 29 December with a detachment of seven sappers and a local guide to destroy a railway bridge near St Arnaud.

"Last flight: this glider, towed by a He 111, took off at the same time as four others tasked with similar missions. In addition to the pilot, it carried seven members of the 3rd company of the Korps Fallschirmpionnier and an Arab Tunisian guide. The glider was towed mainly at 10,000ft, the cable being detached near St Arnaud at around 6,000ft while the aircraft was flying at around 120km/h. The glider landed well but the eight saboteurs were captured before they could reach their objective. Unit: the pilot and his glider had been attached to 5./StG 3 from July to September 1942. Hence the aircraft code S7.

"A few gliders, probably one per Gruppe, were operating with Stukageschwader 3 at this time to bring supplies from Tobruk to the Mersa Matruh region. From October to December 1942, the pilot was based in Trapani but, around 20 December, he was towed with other gliders by Ju 52 to Tunis. After a few days, he was towed by a He 111 to Bizerte, where he arrived on 29 December. He was then to take part in its first and only military operation.

* **Career:** the POW trained as a glider pilot and had been flying gliders for just one year. He only flew gliders and nothing larger than the DFS 230. His licence dates from 9 July 1942."
* **Name:** Flieger Heinz Grimm.
* **Place and date:** near Tebessa (Algeria) 30 December 1942 at around 4am.
* **Type:** DFS 230 glider.
* **Unit:** attached to 11./JG 53.
* **Mission:** took off around midnight to destroy a railway bridge 5km south-east of La Meskiasa, near Tebessa. Only this glider with its nine passengers was assigned to this mission. The group landed and successfully completed the mission. Shortly afterwards, however, it was intercepted. One soldier was killed, while the pilot and eight other soldiers were captured. The soldiers appear to have been from the 4th Company of the 111th Engineer Battalion, known as 'Battalion von Koenen'.
* **Pilot:** Gefr Günter Hahnfeld.

According to one source, the company leader, Oblt Friedrich, and a Tunisian guide managed to slip past the guards by jumping from a moving lorry, then returned to their lines.

This series of sabotage missions was carried out by glider pilots attached to combat units (StG 3 and JG 53). This suggests, if we take into account the pilots and gliders flown on 26 December, that this type of operation was repeated, probably exceeding the number of ten – and perhaps even 20 – at the end of 1942. Unfortunately, not all of them are known.

This DFS 230 has fallen more or less intact into enemy hands.

A DFS 230 found by the British on a captured airfield.

A DFS 230 attached to I./StG 3 in Africa. Note the 'Münchner Löwenbräu' emblem — photo taken during the second half of 1942. VIA PAUL STIPDONK

Quasada, late 1942. A DFS 230 has delivered supplies for StG 3.

7

THE 'KESSEL' BATTLES AND THE KUBAN

DESPITE THE introduction of 'motorised' gliders such as the Go 244, the simple and conventional DFS 230 glider was still being used intensively as late as mid-1942, especially in support of the Wehrmacht's major summer offensive to the east—Fall Blau. As this 'Case Blue' focused on a push towards the Caucasus (southern sector), glider units engaged in other parts of the Eastern Front were initially less affected.

a) Verbindungskommando 1 (northern sector)

This was the case for the 6. DFS 230 Staffel led by Lt Lothar Reich and formed in Hildesheim. By rail, it reached Riga-Spilve where, redesignated 1. (DFS)/VK (S) 1, it was mainly involved in supplying Pleskau (Pskov) and Gatchina on the Leningrad front. Three of its aircraft were loaned for a time to NAG 11 and a detachment was stationed at Siverskaya.

The 1. (Go)/VK (S) 1 was formed with the glider crews engaged shortly before at Kholm as its nucleus. Under the command of Oblt Ehrard Werner, the Staffel (comprising 15 gliders) operated in the same way from Riga.

The official list of losses (which is certainly incomplete) mentions very few among these two units. But this was not entirely inaccurate, as the Wehrmacht remained solid in the northern sector. In October, both Staffeln were recalled to the Reich. Gotha 242 was included in I./LLG 2, while the DFS 230 Staffel disbanded... only to be reformed and sent back to Riga!

At the beginning of December 1942, Oblt Walter Dittmar's 2. (DFS)/VK S 1 arrived in Riga to begin combined training with infantrymen in preparation for an airborne assault on Kronstadt, the famous and powerful Soviet naval base. Like so many other plans of this type, this operation was short-lived and the two DFS 230 squadrons at Riga were merged in February 1943.

b) Verbindungskommando V (central sector)

The 7. DFS 230 Staffel of Oblt Hans Richter comprised 15 DFS 230s and two He

46s. At the end of May, the Staffel reached Smolensk, where it was redesignated 1. (DFS)/VK (S) V. At this airfield, the members of the unit rubbed shoulders with their comrades from 1. (Go)/VK (S) 1, which had 15 Go 242s as well as six He 111s. With the danger of partisans very real, liaison flights were usually made along railway lines (reasonably well defended), to limit the risk of landing in 'partisan' territory. Despite these hazards, life would have been more or less 'routine' for the two glider units – which the casualty list seems to confirm.

c) Verbindungskommando (S) 4 (southern sector)

On 28 June 1942, Fall Blau was launched towards the Caucasus. The German ground troops were supported by 1,200 aircraft from Luftflotte 4. Within this air fleet, three 'conventional' glider Staffeln were identified, including one equipped with the DFS 230:

* 1. (Go)/VK (S) 4 (Hptm Burek);
* 1. (Go)/VK (S) 4 (Oblt Hoffmann);
* 1. (DFS)/VK (S) 4 (Hptm Johann Faè).

To these must be added three other glider Staffeln: 1. (DFS)/VIII (Oblt Schmidt) directly dependent on VIII. Fliegerkorps; 1. (Go)/Lw.Kdo Don (Oblt Wilhelm Kalthoff) operating from Kharkiv with its 15 Go 242s and 1. (DFS)/Lw.Kdo.Don (Oblt Helmut Sannek).

1. (DFS)/VK (S) 4 came from II./LLG 1. Its DFS 230s were not loaded onto wagons but flown out of Hagenow. However, due to a lack of tow aircraft, half a dozen Ju 52s had to tow three gliders at the same time, the one in the centre having a 40m cable and the other two an 80m cable. This 'ad-hoc' approach (reminiscent of British propaganda at the time of Merkur) confirmed the 'poverty' of Luftwaffe transport units, which were forced to engage in dangerous improvisations. Despite the difficulties of the flight, all the gliders made it to Nikolajev, before being shared out between various units for refuelling. The Staffel then moved on to Kharkiv and Zaporozhie.

Gefr Behnke recalled: "For my part, I was assigned to 3. (H)/13. I flew continuously from Kartmyschik-Nem near Simferopol to the Kerch Strait on supply missions. My tug was an Hs 126 from the unit. I transported spare parts, food, technical personnel, etc. and I brought back wounded men or men going on leave from the Staffel. All these flights were treated as combat missions because we were operating within the range of Soviet fighters. I was forced to land in the steppe on several occasions. But each time, my glider was recovered. In autumn 1942, 3. (H)13 was sent to Wollosowo, some 30km from Leningrad. I then crossed the whole of the USSR twice, flying from the Crimea to Wollosovo..."

The second DFS 230 unit sent to support the 1942 summer offensive in the southern sector of the front was 1. (DFS)/VIII. Fl.K. The Staffel trained at Langendiebach under Staka Oblt Schmidt and the pilots flew their gliders to the front in stages departing Germany on 31 May, while the ground crews travelled by train via Vienna, Warsaw and Minsk. Friedrich Zitzmann's diary of that summer noted:

13 June 1942 – Arrival at Kursk. Transfer by lorry over dusty roads under a broiling sun to our first field strip.
16 June – We move to Ochotschevka, our second airstrip.
26 June – Strafing attack by Soviet fighters. No casualties, but some gliders are damaged.
28 June – Start of the offensive. At 0200 the Stuka Staffeln to which we are attached (StG 2 'Immelmann') are airborne. Among

the pilots are Major Dr Kupfer and Oblt Rudel. We are to transport food, clothing, munitions, bombs and fuel supplies. On the return to base we bring back the wounded.

11 July – Departure for Makeyevka. The mechanics fly with us as Bordmechaniker (flight engineers) on our sorties. Numerous repairs are carried out on the gliders as a result of enemy action and sudden changes in temperature, which distort the wings and the tailplane.

19 August – Departure in formation for Zaparosche via Kharkov.

11 September – A large part of the unit is assigned to Hptm Faë's 1. (DFS)/VK (S) 4.

23 September – Flights by Ju 52 to Mariupol then, the next day, to Elista (Kalmuck Steppe). End of October: return to Zaparosche.

By December 1942 the situation had changed drastically in the East. The pockets at Demyansk and Cholm – in the northern sector of the front between Leningrad and Moscow – were still being supplied by an extensive air transport operation following Red Army thrusts which had left German forces surrounded.

As Lufttransportführer (LTF – air transport leader) Morzik put it in his post-war account: "The supplying of these encircled positions represented a new field of endeavour for the air transport units... the 'success' of the resupply operations into Demyansk and Cholm – while not necessarily involving the DFS 230 Staffeln to the same extent that the Gothas were deployed – led 'Germany's military leaders to hold the fundamentally erroneous view that even quite large forces could be resupplied from the air if encircled by the enemy."

Losses of transport aircraft and gliders (mostly

This DFS 230 is transporting an 'outsize' load strapped along the outside of the fuselage — a replacement aileron. VIA PAUL STIPDONK

A Ju 87 D-2 of StG 3 and DFS 230s attached to the unit, operating on the southern sector of the Eastern Front during the summer of 1942. The D-2 had a cable attachment for towing a glider.

This DFS 230 is attached to the Stukageschwader — note the 'S7' Geschwader Kennung. SELLHORN VIA DAVIS

A DFS 230 has landed on Moujik farmlands somewhere in the East. Note the folding hood behind the cockpit has been left open.

This DFS 230 has been wrecked following a heavy landing in one of the numerous pockets kept 'open' in the East. Note the barbed wire wrapped around the landing skid. The bracing supports are visible inside the wing.

DFS 230s at Smolensk in white distemper Wintertarnung.

Ju 52s and Go 242s) at Demyansk and Cholm amounted to hundreds of aircraft.

On 19 December 1942, the Red Army launched a counteroffensive towards Vitebsk and Velikie Louki, the latter being vital for German communications. The Kessel ('cauldron' or 'pocket') formed on 26 December and Velikie Louki was completely surrounded. KG 53, KG 4 and other combat units formed the 'Gefechtsverband Wilke' in an attempt to break the Soviet stranglehold, but also to supply the surrounded and besieged Germans. Gliders were needed, of course, but the Soviets, who had been able to appreciate the 'nuisance' potential of the Lastensegler since the fighting at Cholm, had strengthened their flak. As a result, glider resupply operations took place mainly at night or at dusk.

Winter camouflaged DFS 230 photographed in Dorpat, Estonia.

Winter camouflaged DFS 230 photographed in Dorpat, Estonia.

DFS 230 with white winter camouflage. The type handbook advised that the MG 34 should only be operated once the glider had been released.

The improvised runway to the east of the pocket therefore had to be lit. During flights, the gliders were connected to the tugs by a 40m cable, while position lights on the wingtips of the He 111s allowed the DFS and Gotha pilots to see the towing aircraft. Flights could also be made when the fog was thick, as the aviators were trained in instrument flying. To shorten distances, the gliders took off from Orcha, around 80km west of Smolensk.

STALINGRAD

By mid-December 1942, as it became clear that the Stalingrad pocket could not be supplied by air as efficiently as Demyansk had been earlier that year, all available transport aircraft were dispatched urgently as reinforcements to Oberst Fritz Morzik, the Lufttransportführer assigned to this Kessel. This included all available gliders, among them Staffeln of DFS 230s.

The glider units present in the USSR at the end of 1942 were almost all still assigned to resupply operations into the Velikié Louki pocket, while the DFS 230 Staffeln were still undergoing reorganisation. According to Jean-Louis Roba: "The Luftwaffe high command, overwhelmed by developments in the military situation, was in a feverish state, and contradictory orders were issued one after the other. For example, I./LLG 2 had left Lechfeld on 10 October 1942 for the USSR to take part in an airborne operation aimed at Astrakhan. The Soviet offensive had upset all plans, and I./LLG 2, faced with the indecision of its commanders, had wearily returned to Lechfeld on 25 November!"

LLG 1, partially dismembered at the beginning of 1942, had begun its reconstitution in mid-42 without its Ju 52s, detached from the Geschwader to take part in resupply missions for the Afrika Korps. Other tugs were added, with I./LLG 1 receiving Do 17s (probably E and F types, the 'flying pencils').

At the same time, the tug pilots of II. Gruppe had converted to the Avia B-534-IV, a Czech-made biplane. The conversion of Hauptmann Gerhard Lange's Übungsgruppe III./LLG 1 (reduced months earlier to just 9./LLG 1) continued, with this Gruppe being reinforced by two new Staffeln (7 and 8./LLG 1) and a staff squadron (Stab III./LLG 1) in Goslar. A IV./LLG 1 was also hastily assembled at the beginning of January using obsolete Arado 65s as tugs!

In late 1942 an Erprobungskommando (flight test unit) designated 17./LLG 1 was activated in Döberitz near Berlin. This Staffel, consisting of paratroopers as well as gliders with aircraft of all types as tugs, tested the stability of the Starrschlepp (rigid cable tow) designed to cope with extreme weather conditions such as the Soviet winter. Night and blind flights were tested throughout December 1942 at Döberitz with He 111s.

Kapitän of the Staffel Lt Eugen Wagner remembered: "I was given the task of raising a combat-ready squadron of DFS 230s with He 111 tugs as soon as possible. It was at Döberitz that I saw for the first time the towing system mounted on the back of a He 111. It was 1m long and seemed to me adequate and solid. One of my fellow pilots had been able to make a few take-offs in this way before and had advised me not to do anything when I left the ground, as everything was done automatically. But, as I intended to follow this advice on my first tow, everything went very wrong.

"The pilot of the He 111 took off at too low a speed and I had some problems to get into his wake. The following flights proved that the runway was inadequate and I advised my young pilots to keep in line and to take to the air as soon as possible so as not to be surprised by the sudden climb of the tug. The DFS was a pleasant machine with many qualities but was rather unstable on occasion when being towed by a fast aircraft like the He 111. We also had to face bad weather at that time, which was very significant at the altitudes we were climbing to. That we managed, in spite of all these hazards, to put together a combat unit so quickly seemed to me to be a 'tour de force'."

A Vorkommando (forward detachment) of LLG 1 was placed under the command of Lt Gerhard Raschke (a veteran of the Albert Canal and Corinth). According to his recollections: "In mid-December 1942, Hptm Walter Kiess was ordered to Luftflotte 4 HQ north of the Sea of Azov. The glider units were to supply the troops in the Stalingrad 'Kessel' from the airfields at Stalino, Taganrog, Rostov and Novotcherkassk. The HQ was to be set up at Makivka near Stalino (before possibly being transferred to Zaporozhie). Transfers eastwards began in early January 1943.

"Units that had already been formed arrived by air; reserve aircraft by train ... Flights were made with cables of 80-100m. There was no communication possible between glider and tug ('...ein Bord-zu-Bordsprechverkehr bestand nicht'). More often than not, the aircraft carried a specialist mechanic from the repair workshops. The Vorkommando (advance detachment) of LLG 1 left Hildesheim on 9 January 1943, but had to land in Staaken because of bad weather. This was followed by one stage after another, each mostly of around 250-350km distance.

"Four days after its departure, the Vorkommando reached Zaporozhie. There was a detachment from VK (S) 4 with DFS 230s and He 111s, which were immediately subordinated to LLG 1 led by Oberst Dr Hans Eggersh ... The advance detachment was then ordered to Zverevo, the headquarters of the Lufttransportführer Stalingrad. During the 200km flight, there was clear winter weather with a cloud deck at 300m. The gliders were released and came into land first, to be immediately stowed away in shelters made of snow and ice alongside the runway."

On 14 January Kiess arrived at von Richthofen's Luftflotte 4 HQ to act as liaison officer with responsibility for glider operations and orders to integrate the gliders into the air resupply missions into the city. According to Robert Forsyth: "Kiess was given short shrift by von Richthofen as to the possibility of glider missions into the city." Kiess accused von Richthofen of being too 'frivolous' with regard to towed aircraft matters but was then himself 'taken aback' by conditions on the ground. For a variety of reasons, DFS 230 sorties into the Stalingrad pocket were rejected as being impractical.

It had already been pointed out the previous month that no airfield in the pocket could accommodate gliders. And, as Morzik would later write, gliders were unsuitable for the task. They would have required specialised repair workshops and stocks of equipment such as wheel sets and cables that the forces on the ground had neither the time nor the resources to organise. Stalled or damaged gliders would, it was feared, clog up the airfields – hampering the take-offs and landings of the Ju 52s, He 111s and other aircraft assigned to these vital missions for the encircled troops. In addition, there were not enough fighters to escort these particularly vulnerable formations.

However, movement orders for the DFS 230 units had long since been transmitted by XI. Fliegerkorps (Student's paratroop and air-landing command) and were then in the process being carried out. On 13 January, a report set out the strength of LLG 1 and how the gliders were then dispersed – 'Stand der Zuführung von Transportflugzeugen zur Luftflotte 4':

* **I./LLG 1:** 32 Do 17s and DFS 230s. 23 were en route from Hildesheim to Warsaw; 9 were flying to Posen.
* **II./LLG 1:** 30 Avia B-534s and DFS 230s. 20 were en route to Kalinovka and 3 to Lemberg. 7 crashed at Vinnitsa, Tomaszów and Deblin.
* **III./LLG 1:** 32 Hs 126 and DFS 230s. 26 flew to Warsaw. 6 were grounded in Warsaw and Posen.
* **IV./LLG 1:** 30 Arado 65 and DFS 230s. 27 flew to Warsaw. 3 were grounded in Warsaw and Posen.

Even as the crews of the DFS 230s and other gliders struggled to arrive within range of the besieged city, they could never have any impact on the catastrophe that struck the 6. Armee. Lastensegler missions were relatively few in number and their losses limited. Deployment of gliders was largely handicapped by airfield congestion, severe weather conditions and the late arrival of units. Resupply flights began in earnest around 21 January – even though the pocket was to capitulate less than two weeks later. As one account put it: "In retrospect, I have to say that all this activity was totally superfluous and produced few positive results. All the measures in favour of Stalingrad were taken far too late. We would have needed at least four more weeks to get everything up and running."

Even though their arrival in the southern sector was far too late, the gliders would soon be committed to other missions.

SUPPLYING THE KUBAN BRIDGEHEAD

The glider units (Go 242, DFS 230 and Me 321) dispatched too late to help supply the 6th Army in Stalingrad, would soon prove their worth after the fall of Kessel.

Following the Soviet counteroffensive, the Wehrmacht was forced to evacuate the Caucasus, with the mass of Heeresgruppe A concentrated in the Kuban bridgehead. With the Kerch Strait blocked by ice, only the air force could resupply this bridgehead (more like a pocket on the coast) and evacuate the soldiers who were to be taken back to Crimea.

VIII. Fl.K. under General Martin Fiebig 'recovered' for this task the gliders sent unsuccessfully to Stalingrad and at the end of January 1943 had available:

* I./LLG 2 (Go 242), GS Kdo 2 (Me 321), VK (S) 4 (Go 242/DFS 230) at Bagerovo.
* I, II, IV and 17./LLG 1 (DFS 230) at Kerch.

All the glider units were brought together under the command of the Kommodore Eggersh, who could count on 95 tow aircraft and 147 gliders, distributed as follows:

* **DFS 230:** 83 (67 airworthy)
* **Go 242:** 61 (57)
* **Me 321:** 3 (3)
* **He 111 Z:** 4 (4)
* **He 111:** 7 (2)
* **Avia B-534:** 15 (12)
* **Hs 126 :** 21 (11)
* **Ar 65:** 22 (17)
* **Do 17:** 26 (19)

As the number of tugs was too small for the task in hand, III./KG 4 and its 20 He 111s were attached to the glider units. Shortly afterwards, 17./LLG 1 (Lt E Wagner) arrived from Döberitz with around a dozen He 111s and the same number of DFS 230s. The transfer from Germany did not go smoothly, as the Staffel suffered some losses due to icing and bad weather.

Refuelling and evacuation operations began on 30 January. They were to last just over two months. The short distance between Crimea and Kuban allowed crews to make several flights a day, which facilitated a much-needed evacuation because, under Soviet pressure, Krasnodar airfield was evacuated in mid-February. Timochewskaja suffered the same fate shortly afterwards. Flights continued from Crimea to Slavyanskaya and Primorsk, a more or less improvised airfield.

According to the recollections of Lt Wagner, Staka of the very recent 17./LLG 1: "Take-offs from a huge, frozen and rutted field strip were always risky. Most of them took place in the early hours of the morning. But over time, the pilots of the He 111 and DFS 230 had gained enough experience to

LLG 1 had around 20 Ar 65s available for this task. Note the DFS 230 has not jettisoned the wheeled dolly. A wheeled landing was possible.

IV. Gruppe of LLG 1 hastily established in early 1942 operated the Arado Ar 65 as a DFS 230 tug. The Luftwaffe actually planned to dispatch these obsolete biplanes to Stalingrad with their Lastensegler to 'participate' in the airlift, although perhaps fortunately for the crews they got no further than Warsaw!

A view from the tug aircraft.

Heinkel He 45 biplane tugs in action.

avoid collisions. The Staffel leaders of the Heinkel and glider units also got on very well, and the tug pilots were particularly competent. Most of them were Oberfeldwebel pilots able to fly on instruments.

"When they were not towing gliders, He 111 crews were involved in special operations such as bombing flak positions. This is how the Staka of the He 111 Staffel, Hptm Ickenroth, was killed with his crew. After carrying out a large number of missions from the Asian part of the USSR, we still had time to try out innovations such as the 'aerial freight train', i.e. two DFS 230s towed in single file by a He 111."

THE LUFTWAFFEN KOMMANDO DON

Although the 'pockets' at Stalingrad and Velikié Louki received the most attention from the Wehrmacht (and from post-war historians), other encirclements took place throughout the harsh winter of 42/43 in the 'southern' sector. These pockets of resistance were supplied by a unit mentioned earlier: the Luftwaffen Kommando Don. The two Staffeln of Go 242s and DFS 230s operating out of Konotop dispersed their aircraft among various units as and when required.

On 13 January 1943, Fw Karl Scheuing of the DFS Staffel supplied the Techerkovo 'Kessel' with no fewer than 37,000 rounds of ammunition for the 8,000 soldiers under siege. After his glider was destroyed on landing, Scheuing fought with the surrounded garrison.

There were other highlights, as another DFS 230 pilot, Gefr Herr, recounted: "On 2 February 1943, I was ordered to supply part of the 2. Armee encircled near Gortschenetschnoje with a cargo of ammunition and hand grenades. I took off from Kharkiv North on a clear day. After an hour's flight, I reached the objective at an altitude of 1,500m. I dropped the cable and flew low over the village before landing in the main street. Everything was well organised."

The glider was quickly unloaded and set on fire. The next day, the pilot took part in the evacuation of the pocket and, after a gruelling ten-day march, was reunited with several pilots from his unit who were also forced to retreat on foot. On 21 February, the escapees returned to Poltava in a Ju 52 and then went back to their unit.

8

LATE 1943 – BACK TO FRANCE AND ITALY

WITH THE disaster at Stalingrad and the expulsion of the Axis from North Africa, the first few months of 1943 saw a 'shift' of glider units from the Eastern Front back to the West. The Fallschirmjäger retrained again as airborne troops for the first time since 'Merkur' having been deployed as 'elite' infantrymen in the USSR. Once again they trained for operational jumps by parachute and precision insertions by glider. The origin of this return to their roots probably lies in Operation Jubilee, the failed landing at Dieppe on 19 August 1942. The fear of invasion was real for the OKW and with the Normandy/Brittany sector under threat, 7. Flieger Parachute Division set up its headquarters there. In this way, the Germans killed two birds with one stone – reinforcing a 'sensitive' region while training their men in what could easily be described as a 'pleasant' environment.

According to paratrooper Lt Martin Pöppel: "On 17 September 1942, we left for France ... We landed at Argentan and went on to Saint-Sever ... We were welcomed by friendly people and I was given a nice room with a large French bed in a requisitioned house ... There was an abundance of food here, the potatoes were very good, the butter was thick and we were served fruit. As we say, you can live like God in France."

According to German paratrooper specialist Jean-Yves Nasse the parachute battalions FJR 1, 3 and 4 were sent to France for rest. These regiments were stationed in Normandy and jump schools (Châteaudun, Dreux, Lyon, Troyes) were set up. Between 1942 and 1943, all these regiments and units carried out rotations in the USSR.

In the early months of 1943, with the situation in the Mediterranean developing very badly, it was soon recognised that the Italians would likely change sides. So-called 'intervention groups' were set up as a 'rapid-reaction' force, hence the revival of airborne units that had seemingly perished in the 'tomb of Crete'.

III./LLG 1 returned from the USSR and was sent to Beaumont-sur-Oise with its DFS 230s, two Do 17s and two Hs 126s. In May 1943, two Staffeln of Do 17 tugs were transferred to I./LLG 1, which moved to Gaël.

I./LLG 2 was reported to have moved to Essey in March 1943. Officially, at least, because, according to the casualty list, this unit (or an advanced detachment?) was already present in Nancy in January.

During early 1943 with snow still on the ground, gliders and tugs started to depart the Eastern Front. A DFS 230 gets airborne behind a Do 17. JAMES V. CROW COLLECTION

Fallschirmjäger training with a DFS 230.

Another unit was operating in France before the arrival of the 'bulk of the troops'. 1 Staffel/ Erprobungskommando IX based at Laval took the name 'Erprobungsgruppe Laval' at the end of April. This group was led by Hptm Heinz Trautwein, ex-Staka of 1./LLG 2 (who was shortly to take charge of II./LLG 1). This Gruppe brought together He 111 and Do 17 tugs as well as DFS 230s from LLG 1. A detachment of parachutists took part in combined exercises with these aircraft.

In November 1942, the 1. Fallschirmjäger-Division (FJD) had been formed in Normandy, with the 2. FJD being set up in Brittany in March 1943. The mass arrival of gliders meant that exercises could be stepped up, but not all went smoothly. On 12 March, for example, a simulated attack on Tours airfield ended in disaster when the parachute of Uffz Albin Weigold's glider failed to deploy fully. The DFS 230 crashed, killing the pilot and passengers.

As the Normandy/Brittany sector had become risky due to the increasing intrusion of enemy fighters, the two parachute divisions were transferred in May to the south of France... which brought them closer to Italy. The HQ of the 1. FJD was at Avignon, that of the 2. FJD at Alès.

The glider units followed:

- I./LLG 1 left Gaël for Lézignan (with 52 Do 17s and 136 DFS 230s)
- III./LLG 1 from Beaumont to Valence (with 32 Hs 126s and 120 DFS 230s)
- I./LLG 2, shared between Essey and Beaumont, reached Orange (with 27 He 111s and 188 Go 242s)

Erpr.Gr. Laval was then disbanded, the He 111s going to Orange while the rest of the aircraft/gliders returned to LLG 1. Since they were to be used in support of the airborne, it goes without saying that the most numerous gliders were DFS 230s, as

A rare view of a DFS 230 equipped with a fixed MG 34 and two roof-mounted MG 15s on special supports providing wide arcs of fire.

can be seen both from the list of personnel and from the losses at the time, since of the 26 gliders damaged or destroyed, only two were Go 242s. The Gothas were nevertheless essential, not only for carrying soldiers, but above all for loading equipment that could not be transported in Ju 52s.

One former 2.FJD paratrooper wrote: "The magnificent landscape of the south of France, with its very mild climate, is one of the most beautiful parts of Europe… The whole country is unique, with orchards and vineyards like those along the Rhine. The battalions and companies were spread out in pleasant barracks. Paratroopers were often housed in tents near rivers or other waterways. When the weather permitted, combat exercises were carried out, [which comprised] jumps from Ju 52 or He 111 aircraft and steep landings in DFS 230 gliders.

"These exercises took place in Avignon and Montélimar. In their spare time, soldiers could visit the pleasant countryside and enjoy its fruit and wine. Cherries and apricots were plentiful.

Preparing for a flight.

They were eaten in the hot sun or sent home. The men swam to their hearts' content in the Gardon and other rivers. They jumped into the crystal-clear water to catch fish with gleaming scales..."

A few units were even lucky enough to enjoy trips to the theatre or cinema. There were also concerts. On 1 June 1943, Generalfeldmarschall Gerd von Rundstedt put the XI. Fliegerkorps on alert due to fears of a landing on the Iberian peninsula. On 23 June, Obstlt Heinrich Trettner, Chief of Staff of XI. Fl.K., issued another alert, this time fearing a landing in France on the Mediterranean coast. But this was not to be.

The members of the glider units enjoyed their stay in what was for them a 'land of milk and honey' just as much as their paratrooper comrades. The casualty lists support this idyllic picture. Very few were killed or wounded during these weeks, although Oblt Bentrup, leading 10./LLG 1, was injured in an accident and two airmen were killed on 24 June at Istres. The latter belonged to the Fallsch-Ln Abt 41, a detachment with around 13 DFS 230s and two Go 242s, assigned to transporting paratroopers' radio and signals equipment.

In June, Lastensegler units in France were reinforced by 17./LLG 1, which had operated shortly before from Kerch. The unit arrived in Orange with no fewer than 69 DFS 230s, where it was renamed DFS-Staffel 23. To compensate for its lack of tugs, Transportgruppe 30 joined it in Orange with 45 He 111s.

The situation changed dramatically in the early hours of 10 July 1943 when Operation Husky, the Allied invasion of Sicily, was launched. The Luftwaffe attempted to set up an air-bridge to transport troops and equipment to the island. To do this, it had the following number of gliders and tugs at its disposal in the south of France:

- **I./LLG 1 (Hptm Hans Krug):** 136 DFS 230s and 52 Do 17s.
- **II./LLG 1 (Hptm Heinz Trautwein):** 23 DFS 230s and 23 Ju 87s. The strength of this Gruppe was very limited, as some Staffeln had been temporarily posted outside France.
- **III./LLG 1 (Hptm Josef Karl):** 120 DFS 230s and 32 Hs 126s.
- **I./LLG 2 (Maj Walter Kroworsch):** 188 Go 242s and 27 He 111s. The list of losses includes very low Go 242 serial numbers (WNr 2, 3, 4, 8, 18, etc.). This would seem to indicate that, in order to build up this Gruppe, a wide range of 'obsolete' aircraft was drawn on.
- **DFS-Staffel 23 (Lt Wagner):** 69 DFS 230s.
- **Fallsch-Ln Abt. 41 (?):** 2 Go 242s, 13 DFS 230s and four Ju 52s.

Over the course of the next two weeks, dozens of gliders and Heinkel tugs were lost as they

Two views of landings with braking parachute deployed. The chute is seen here flaring to stop the glider in as short a distance as possible.

Nose-mounted braking rockets installed on a DFS 230.

attempted to bring reinforcements and supplies into Sicily. Meanwhile the large transport force of several hundred aircraft assembled by the Luftwaffe in the south of France had not gone unnoticed by the Allies. On 17 August 1943 – the same day as the 'notorious' Schweinfurt-Regensburg bombing raid – USAF bomber formations based in North Africa hit airfields in the south of France, packed with transport aircraft and gliders. According to author Guy Julien: "On 17 August, almost 600 Luftwaffe transport aircraft and gliders were stationed on the airfields of the lower Rhône valley. By late July, the Allies were well aware that a veritable air bridge was being set up, with the airfields of south-eastern France at its hub ... This accumulation of air resources led the Allies to mount a raid designed to eradicate this threat at a time when preparations for the future landings in Campania and Apulia were in full swing."

At 0930 that morning the 99th Bomb Group took off from the Oudna, followed by the 301st BG, also based at Oudna, who launched 50 four-engined aircraft. The last USAF bombers to leave African soil were the 40 aircraft of the 2nd BG based at Massicault, near Bizerte. The NASAF (Northwest African Strategic Airforce) committed an armada of around 200 B-17s, almost all the resources of the 5th Bomb Wing that formed its spearhead.

The mission assigned to them on that fine August Thursday was to strike the airfields at Istres and Salon, with the aim not so much to damage the installations as to destroy the enemy's air potential by causing maximum losses among the crews, which the intelligence services estimated could not be reconstituted for a long time. To this end, the planes were armed with small 10kg M-1 cluster bombs. It was just after 1230 when the 99th BG reached the Initial Point off Port St Louis du Rhône. From there, the group headed straight for Istres. A quarter of an hour later, passing in turn over the same point, the B-17s of the 97th BG turned towards Salon.

Lt Busse, a veteran of Crete and at that time with I./LLG 1, experienced this attack on the ground: "Departure order for Istres. We already know this airfield. It is the biggest in Europe, with a surface area of 6km by 6km, a flat expanse with no concrete runways. In other words, a vast plain without trees or obstacles. We landed at Istres and received orders to get ready to leave as soon as possible. The detachments set up in their allocated places. The technical staff were busy checking the aircraft and supplying them with fuel and ammunition. The cables are attached.

"Shortly before departure, I contemplate the sky. Any mistral to worry about? No, but a few very high contrails streak the blue sky. Our aircraft? Doubtful. Enemy scouts, then. That doesn't bode well ... The day dawned under a scorching sun and very quickly the temperature rose. We move to our position. With our mechanics, we are close to our aircraft. But there's still an hour to go, and we're going to spend it in the shade cast by the wings of our gliders. Suddenly, the air raid warning sounded. Everything came to a head when we saw imposing condensation trails coming from the south. Where could we hide?

"Those close to the buildings ran for it. But what about us? And, from the south, a huge white trail following an imposing formation of bombers growing ever larger. I look around desperately in all directions. It would be madness to hide in the glider or the Do 17s. Then I saw some pipes dug into the ground and covered with concrete slabs. We threw ourselves into this 50cm high improvised shelter and waited, our noses in the mud. We heard explosions: cluster bombs, exploding aircraft, detonating ammunition, etc. When the attack was over, we climbed out of the ditch.

"The sight was disastrous. Wrecked machines, gliders with their wings holed, scattered bodies... We gathered up the dead and took them to a hangar. There wasn't enough room for everyone. Some are unidentifiable. Our unit had been struck in the heart. The next day, the airfield was cleared, an inventory was made of the aircraft in good condition and an attempt was made to identify the dead. The mechanics set about repairing as many aircraft as possible. Each unit was then ordered to return to its home base. We left for Lézignan without having been able to go on an operation. Supplies to Italy were compromised..."

At least 100 gliders – around 50 DFS 230s and 40 Gothas – were destroyed in the 17 August attack. Of course by this stage Sicily had fallen, the Germans had fallen back across the Straits of Messina and the Allies were preparing landings along the southern Italian coast. Mussolini had been arrested and Italy was about to change sides and join the Allies. All of which led directly to another infamous 'coup de main' for the Luftwaffe's DFS 230 glider force.

Bombs rain down on Istres airfield. Note the large numbers of DFS 230s parked up towards the top of the image. Towards the bottom of the image it is possible to make out two of the massive five-engined He 111 Zwilling tugs.

DFS 230s and Do 17 tug at an airfield in the south of France during the early summer of 1943, possibly Valence or Orange.

Wer im Herzen seiner Lieben lebt,
der ist nicht tot, der ist nur fern.

DEM ANDENKEN
IM GEBETE
an den tapferen Helden

Karl Neumeier

Unteroffizier und Flugzeugführer

Geboren am 14. August 1920 in Wiedergeltingen; für's Vaterland durch Flugunfall gestorben am 28. August 1943 und auf dem Heldenfriedhof in Carcasonne (Südfrankreich) beerdigt.

Schwer war schon der Trennungsschmerz,
Jetzt aber bricht uns fast das Herz.
Als Held starbst du für uns zu früh,
Vergessen werden wir dich nie.
Wir können dir nun nichts mehr bieten,
Mit nichts mehr dich erfreu'n,
Nicht einmal eine Hand voll Blüten
Auf deinen Hügel streu'n!
Wir konnten dich nicht sterben seh'n,
Und nicht an deinem Grabe steh'n.
Fern ist dein Grab, tief unser Schmerz,
Doch ruhe sanft, du treugeliebtes Herz.

O Herr, gib ihm die ewige Ruhe
und das ewige Licht leuchte ihm!

Uffz Karl Neumeier of I./LLG 1 was killed at Lézignan in a DFS 230 on 28 August 1943. His civilian glider pilot's insignia (Segelflieger Abzeichen) can be seen on his tunic.

Personnel from a LLG 1 Staffel position the landing gear of DFS 230 before hitching up the glider to a Do 17 tug.

Generalmajor Kurt Student, commander of XI. Fliegerkorps, reviews the personnel of Luftlandgeschwader 1. On his left is Oberst Dr Hans Eggersh, Kommodore of LLG 1. ECPA-D

DFS 230s towed by Avia B-534s of LLG 1's Sondergruppe over France. ECPA-D

A Czech Avia B.534 tug of the Sondergruppe LLG 1 is pushed into position at Lézignan-Corbières. The Sondergruppe was established for missions in Italy and disbanded in September 1943. WOLFGANG STOCKER, ECPA-D

"Since sunrise, the parachutists' camp resembled a disturbed anthill". Eating breakfast at an airfield occupied by LLG 1. The Fallschirmer bivouacked on their airfields. Note the Kapok life-jackets for a long flight over water. ECPA-D

Hptm Josef Karl, Kommandeur of III./LLG 1 (right in photo), prepares to land at Valence airfield (Drôme), where the Gruppe was stationed. Karl was one of the glider pilots involved in Operation Merkur. ECPA-D

The DFS 230 and Dornier Do 17 pilots of III./LLG 1 listen attentively to the briefing given by the Kommandeur. ECPA-D

9

OPERATION EICHE – GRAN SASSO AND THE RESCUE OF MUSSOLINI

NO ACCOUNT of the combat history of the DFS 230 can avoid detailing the 'infamous' 'Unternehmen Eiche' (Operation Oak), the rescue of Mussolini. Although in the end opposition was minimal, it was an operation made possible by the DFS 230 which will be remembered – albeit in a largely exaggerated manner – as cementing the 'reputation' of SS Hauptsturmführer Otto Skorzeny – 'an SS-propaganda coup'.

In his memoirs, published shortly after the war, Skorzeny describes how on 25 July 1943 he was urgently called to Adolf Hitler's headquarters. He was presented to the Führer along with other 'adventurers' and was singled out for two reasons: he had travelled through Italy on a motorbike in 1934 and... he was Austrian like Hitler. In short, he knew the Italians but distrusted them, having, like many of his compatriots, always refused to support the Italian annexation of Alto Adige (South Tyrol).

Hitler informed him of Mussolini's arrest on the same day and his desire to free him. The Führer foresaw the forthcoming Italian volte-face and the handing over of the Duce to the Allies. Together with Kurt Student, Skorzeny flew to Rome where he met Kesselring, and welcomed a small detachment of his men who had also arrived by air along with elements of Fallschirmjäger-Regiment 7 on their way to the south of the Italian boot.

The German secret services and a small group of trusted men around Skorzeny searched frantically for the Duce's place of detention. They relied on gossip, listened to the 'confidences' of Italian officers, paid informers, etc. Mussolini was sometimes reported as being held on a cruiser, sometimes in the Apennines, sometimes in Sardinia, sometimes on an islet near Elba, etc. The Italian secret services seemed to be doing their utmost to mislead their German counterparts. But at the beginning of September, according to Skorzeny: "My small personal intelligence service brought us absolute certainty: Benito Mussolini was interned, well guarded, in a mountain hotel in the Gran Sasso range."

On 8 September 1943, the Austrian and his second-in-command took off in a He 111 from Pratica di Mare to fly over the Gran Sasso mountain range and photograph the Campo Imperatore hotel, where the Duce was being held. On their return, they learned of the Italian 'change-of-sides'. The days that followed were feverish and confused.

Some Italians had indeed laid down their arms... Badoglio's government had not seen fit to declare war on its erstwhile ally (it would not do so until 13 October). But in Rome, in other Italian cities and in the Balkans, Italian soldiers quickly opened fire on their former German comrades. Bloody fighting broke out everywhere.

The chaos made it difficult to hold meetings and, according to Skorzeny, the photos were not studied until 10 September. The Hauptsturmführer declared that he had chosen a triangular meadow close to the hotel, which would allow gliders to land: "It was then that the Chief of Staff of the Fallschirmjäger corps was assigned to us as experts for this airborne operation. They were against my plan. They were of the opinion that an airborne operation at this altitude and without a prepared landing field would be technically unfeasible. They also thought that this type of landing would cause around 80% casualties. The remaining troop numbers would be too small to have any chance of success. I defended my opinion. After due consideration, General Student gave his final approval. Twelve gliders were to be launched immediately from the south of France towards Rome. The date set was 12 September."

Skorzeny's account seems to be contradicted by the report of Oblt Johannes Heidenreich, Staka of 12./LLG 1: the Sonderstaffel Heidenreich took off from Valencia on 8 September 1943 at 0856 and flew to Ottana (Sardinia) in stages: Saint Raphaël, Pisa, Grosseto, Venafiorita. The tug aircraft were Hs 126s with limited range. It is likely that this Staffel was activated on the 8th to take part in the operation to free the Duce, who was then thought to be held in the Sardinian sector. Skorzeny's 'original idea' is therefore somewhat questionable...

Still according to Heidenreich: "The Staffel reached Grosseto the same day at 1758 with 11 tug-glider Schleppzüge. A twelfth was forced to land in Sarzana. Two others had to temporarily remain in Pisa following slight damage to the gliders. On September 11 at 1800, the Sonderstaffel received the order to fly to Pratica di Mare ... There were some difficulties due to the rough nature of this airfield but ten teams were able to achieve it ... At Pratica, I dispersed the aircraft and gliders, putting them under cover to limit damage in the event of an air attack ... Around 1030, a meeting was held with Hstuf Skorzeny, Oblt Georg von Berlepsch and various paratrooper officers. Hptm Langguth detailed the aerial photos for us. I assigned the glider pilots according to landing locations."

According to Skorzeny, "the pilots and group leaders, Hauptsturmführer SS Menzel, Obersturmführer SS Radl, Scharführer SS Schwert, Oblt von Berlepsch and eight other group leaders of the paratroopers were gathered in a room where General Student made a rather short presentation according to which, in all cases, only a 'skid' or 'sliding' landing was permitted. Any attempt to come in on a steep vertical approach was prohibited because of the special danger it presented."

Indeed, due to the strong winds on the Gran Sasso and the impossibility of correctly using the braking parachute, only more or less horizontal landings were possible. Skorzeny adds in his account that it was he who gave the practical instructions to the pilots – which was probably unlikely. The operation almost failed to get underway at 1210 following an air raid alert. According to Skorzeny, bombs fell on the airfield but did not hit any aircraft. Heidenreich, for his part, does not mention this. The Henschel 126s were quickly refuelled (some partially) and the men boarded.

Skorzeny resumes his story: "We boarded our gliders and sat astride the narrow bench serving as a seat. We were packed together like sardines. There was barely enough space left for our armament ... I gave the signal for takeoff. The engines roared. We gained altitude slowly, describing large circles. The glider formation headed north-east. The weather seemed ideal for our business. Great white clouds hung in the skies at 3,000m. If they stayed in place, we could arrive almost unnoticed.

"We could hardly move. I noticed that the soldier behind me was starting to get sick ... He began to vomit but fortunately into a cap handed to him by a comrade ... The pilot kept us informed about the relative positions of the aircraft. From inside the DFS, you could barely see anything of the landscape. The small side windows were almost opaque and the slits were too small. The DFS 230 was an airy machine – a few steel tubes covered with canvas. We didn't appear to have made much progress on this point, as surely an aluminium fuselage would have been more 'elegant'. We flew through a cloud more imposing than the others to reach the altitude of 3,500m. For a short moment, everything was grey around us. Soon we came out into bright sunshine. We were above the clouds..."

The crew of the Henschel then reported by radio that two tug-glider teams were missing. According to Skorzeny, they were in an accident during take-off but Heidenreich, who flew as an observer in one of the Hs 126 tugs, specified that a Rotte took the wrong direction, suggesting that the mission was abandoned. Heidenreich, however, was not fooled and continued on his way, leading the other Hs 126/DFS 230 'teams' in his wake. Skorzeny claims to have taken command of the formation at that moment: "Using my paratrooper's dagger, I cut fist-sized holes in the fabric of the fuselage to get a glimpse of the exterior. I was happy enough then at the age of the gliders and their canvas covering against which I had just railed."

As the gliders approached their objective, the wind gusts increased in strength and the clouds grew thicker. The aircraft appeared over the Gran Sasso coming from the sun. At 1403 the first glider detached and flew as planned over the mountain hotel. The others followed at very short intervals. They now had to come in and land in the meadow located a few dozen metres from the hotel.

According to Skorzeny: "I shouted, 'Helmets on.' The hotel appeared below us. Our tow cable was dropped. We were suddenly surrounded by a silence disturbed only by the whistling of the wind on the wings of the glider. The pilot described a wide circle searching the gently sloping meadow, the designated landing spot..."

It was then realised that the meadow was much more rugged than the photos taken by Skorzeny aboard the He 111 had led the raiders to believe. Lt Elimar Meyer, pilot of the DFS 230 in which the Hauptsturmführer was flying, elected at that point – and based on his experience – to embark on the prohibited manoeuvre: diving more or less vertically while triggering the opening of the braking parachute.

He left a very detailed account of the mission: "We flew over the first heights east of Rome, the foothills of the Sabine Mountains. The formation headed continuously eastwards, gradually gaining altitude. Half hidden by the clouds, the Gran Sasso mountains appeared ahead of us. Three-quarters of our flight time is up. Quickly one last look at the map and the aerial photo. The little black dot in front must be the Campo Imperatore. With my left hand, I release the cable, the tractor plane disappears in a dive and I immediately feel the nose of my glider pointing downwards. I decide not follow the instructions given by Skorzeny –besides, why was a passenger giving me the pilot orders on how to fly my mission? In any case, where he's sitting, he can't see anything.

"The point becomes clearer. It's a big building. I use the rudder pedals to position myself well, but the swirling winds against the rock walls make my task difficult. I managed to fly over the building – there is no sign of life. Is it abandoned? Suddenly, four faces appeared at a window. If they are soldiers they are probably surprised by the arrival of these unknown aircraft. I then discovered that the flat land 'identified' by the aerial photos was in fact sloping and stony. I make my decision directly. I turn very sharply, pinning the crew and passengers in their seats and throw my glider on the ground while braking as hard as possible. For a second I close my eyes and am unable to think. There is a final shock more brutal than the others. The machine reared up on its nose. We had landed.

"The door was thrown open and the first soldier was already outside. I dropped down from the cockpit, weapon in hand, next to the glider. We were 15m from the hotel. All around us the rocky terrain slowed down our machine very quickly but had wrecked it in the process. Our landing to a standstill took less than 20m. The braking chute billowing out behind us slowly collapsed..."

A little behind them, Fw Heiner Lohrmann landed some 300m from the hotel. There were only about 60 men, pilots included, heading towards the Duce's 'prison'. The rest of the story is well known. The effect of surprise and the FG 42s (FJR automatic assault rifles) compensated for the numerical superiority of the enemy (some 150 Italian soldiers). "Mani in alto!" (Hands up!). In a few minutes, the unmotivated Carabinieri had laid down their arms and the hotel was in the hands of the Fallschirmjäger, practically without combat and without loss of life.

Skorzeny then entered Mussolini's room and declared: "Duce, der Führer schickt mich! Sie sind frei!" The hotel being connected to the valley by a cable car, a large detachment of paratroopers simultaneously captured the lower station to prevent any sending of Italian reinforcements. However, bringing Mussolini down by cable car was risky. A Fi 156, piloted by Hptm Heinrich Gerlach, Student's pilot in the XI. Fl.K., made a straightforward landing on the plateau to evacuate the Duce. At which point Skorzeny took the initiative of climbing into the Storch.

His huge frame and weight added to that of Gerlach and the passenger, together with the short takeoff 'track' made the next stage of the operation unnecessarily risky. But the SS officer did not budge. Evidently the Austrian feared, if Mussolini arrived alone in Berlin, that the glory of his liberation would be attributed to the daring action of the paratroopers alone.

With this additional ballast, the Fieseler Stork launched into a potentially deadly dive off the side of the mountain. Pilot Gerlach barely succeeded in pulling it up. Once in front of the Führer, Skorzeny monopolised the 'glory'; praised by the propaganda services, he was rewarded with the Ritterkreuz. Meanwhile, on the Gran Sasso, the airborne personnel dismantled the onboard equipment of the 12 DFS 230s before setting fire to the airframes. They couldn't be flown out of course and the impacts with the rocky ground mostly destroyed or seriously damaged them. One pilot was injured. The airborne troops came down into the valley using the cable car.

At a ceremony held a few days later, Hptm Heinrich Gerlach was awarded the Ritterkreuz, as was Lt Elimar Meyer, the pilot of Skorzeny's glider. Although he subtly took the lion's share of the credit, the Austrian was not averse to sharing the 'spotlight'. Oblt Georg von Berlepsch, who led the paratroopers of 1./FJR 7, received the Deutsches Kreuz in Gold (he was killed on 2 February 1944 during the fighting at Nettuno), as did the Staka of 12./LLG 1, Oblt Johannes Heidenreich, and two DFS 230 pilots, Ofw Hans Neelmeyer and Uffz Gustav Thielmann. In his report, Heindenreich lists the names of the other glider pilots: Uffz Karl-Heinz Ronsdorf (wounded), Fw Heiner Lohrmann, Ofw Beerenboldt, Uffz Maier, Uffz Jenniches, Uffz Gedenk and Uffz Stark.

As Jean-Louis Roba explained: "Soon after the end of the war, the in-demand Otto Skorzeny wrote his successful memoir. He soon became 'Mussolini's liberator' for the media and the general public. Yet his account is full of fabrications: in addition to his astonishing foresight and knowledge of the DFS 230, it was he who 'instructed the pilots', it was he who 'took charge of the air formation', it was he who 'ordered Meyer to drop the cable at the right moment', and so on.

"In his own account, Elimar Meyer has done justice to many of these 'exaggerations'. Without the parachutists, Skorzeny would never have been able to free Mussolini and, without the DFS 230

Elements of the 1 Kompanie of Fallschirmjäger-Regiment 7 and the Sondergruppe of LLG 1 photographed after the raid by PK Berichter Toni Schneiders.

glider pilots, the parachutists would never have been able to surprise Mussolini's jailers. Skorzeny later received an angry letter from the Fallschirmjäger Association criticising him for playing down the vital role of the airborne pilots. The Austrian replied with a letter of apology stating that this had never been his intention. But despite this, SS Hauptsturmführer Otto Skorzeny will remain for posterity (and as the Propagandastaffel had wanted) the impetuous leader of the Reich's commandos, the only hero of the Gran Sasso."

Six days after the success of Operation Eiche, DFS 230 Lastensegler units in the Mediterranean were dealt a final blow when USAAF bombers raided Pratica di Mare airfield, which was crowded with Ju 52s and transport aircraft of all types. The attack was just as destructive as the raid on Istres one month earlier. LLG 1 lost 12 aircraft (Do 17, Hs 126 and Avia 534) and three others were damaged. Thirty-six DFS 230s were destroyed and 21 damaged. Although not specified in the casualty list, seven pilots were killed (probably members of the crews of tow aircraft). With the evacuation of the islands, the glider force was surplus to requirements and ordered back to France.

An unidentified pilot of 12./LLG 1, who took part in the successful operation.

In tow behind a Henschel Hs 126.

Freed, Mussolini (black coat and hat) is photographed with his liberators... and his jailers. Tall and imposing, Skorzeny is clearly recognisable to his right even though he is wearing a Luftwaffe uniform rather than that of the SS.

Two views of 'LC + 1-8', probably the DFS 230 piloted by Lt Elimar Meyer of 1./LLG 1 with SS Hauptsturmführer Otto Skorzeny on board. Meyer flew the DFS 230 to within 15m of the Campo Imperatore hotel, where the Duce was being held.

The 'famous' propaganda photo — a parachutist of 1./FJR 7 at Gran Sasso with the rare FG Fallschirmjägergewehr 42 machine gun of the German paratroopers.

Les parachutistes qui se sont distingués lors de l'expedition du GranSasso, reçoivent la croix de chevalier des mains du Général des Aviateurs STUDENT

En reconnaissance de son héroisme dans la lutte pour l'avenir de notre peuple, le Führer a décoré le général d'aviation Kurt Student, comme 305ème soldat de l'Armée allemande, de la

FEUILLE DE CHÊNE
DE LA CROIX DE CHEVALIER
DE LA CROIX DE FER

Le nom de ce général a été mentionné la dernière fois dans les communiqués relatant la libération du Duce. Ce sont en effet, des troupes de parachutistes, soumises à ses ordres, qui ont participé à cet acte d'éclat

Capitaine GERLACH

Sous-lieutenant MEYER

The Luftwaffe magazine *Der Adler* reports on the award ceremony for the Gran Sasso fighters. Generalmajor Kurt Student presents the Knight's Cross to Meyer, the DFS 230 pilot, and Gerlach, who flew Mussolini off the mountain in the Fi 156.

Gerlach, Student's personal pilot, and Meyer receive the Ritterkreuz, the aircraft pilot wearing the Stahlhelm while the glider pilot wears the parachutist helmet.

Three airmen from 12./LLG 1 are awarded the DKiG.

An Italian vehicle used to position a DFS 230.

This photo series was taken by Propaganda-Kompanie Bildberichter Wolfgang Stocker with 8./LLG 1. The Staffel spent a month training in Norway in late 1943. Here at Banak airfield, Luftlandegeschwader 1 personnel gear up for an exercise over the airfield while playing with the unit's Staffelhund — dog mascot — which is passed up into the DFS-230 coded 'LB+1-97'.

The Feldwebel holding the dog is Günther Naumann of the Fallschirmjäger Kriegsberichterzug or airborne propaganda section. He held the combat clasp for airborne or transport units (Frontflugspange), as well as the Iron Cross and the radio gunner's brevet (Bordschütze). The tractor tug is a Ford-Ferguson 9N with its radiator exposed. Note the nose-art on the DFS in the lower image — 'Sieg' or 'victory'. Reporter Stocker was killed in Italy during 1944. More of his images can be seen on the ECPA-D website (http://imagesdefensegouv.fr). WOLFGANG STOCKER ECPA-D FALLAOK F1537/52/97. COURTESY NICOLAS FERARD

10

OPERATION 'RÖSSELSPRUNG' – KNIGHT'S MOVE AGAINST TITO

As already mentioned, at the end of October 1943, 10. and 12./LLG 1 had been brought together in an 'Einsatzgruppe LLG 1' based in Siena. On 6 and 7 February 1943, two teams from 12./LLG 1 fell victim to Allied fighters. One author wrote of the deadly encounter on the 7th: "Four Spitfire MK Vc of the 4th FS/52nd FG took off for a reconnaissance of enemy shipping on the Toulon-Genoa route. After an uneventful flight, the Spitfires, flying at 8,000ft, crossed paths with four Hs 126s at around 9.15am off Loano, two of which were towing DFS 230 gliders. This would have been a small formation of 12./LLG 1 returning to Nancy from Avignon. Lieutenants Canning and Burnett shot down the tugs and gliders on their first pass, while Lieutenants Bishop and McCampbell claimed the other two Henschels. However, the glycol tank of Canning's Spitfire was hit by his victim's defensive fire, forcing the American pilot to parachute into enemy territory."

The official list of losses shows only one glider that day and no Henschels (but the list may not be complete). In any case, the two gliders mentioned above took their first mechanic (1. Wart) with them, clear signs of a transfer. It was around this date that the DFS 230s returned to Nancy. Shortly afterwards, III./LLG 1 went to Serbia. A few days later, II./LLG 1 left Lorraine (temporarily Germanised) for Zagreb. The two Gruppen reinforced the Schleppgruppe 1 gliders already present in the Balkans. Schleppgruppe 1 had evolved somewhat since its formation at the end of 1943, while at the same time dispersing its components. Hptm Walter Dittmar's Schleppgruppe 1 saw its strength increased in December:

* 1. (DFS) 1 (Oblt Lehmann) had four Hs 126s and 17 DFS 230s.
* 2. (DFS) 1 (Hptm Josef Wagener) had six He 45s and 17 DFS 230s.

These two DFS 230 Staffeln flew transport missions as far afield as Salonika and Bucharest, as well as visiting Tirana and Zagreb. Gradually, the obsolete He 45s were replaced by Ju 87s. Due to a lack of space at Semlin, the DFS Staffeln were moved to Samos (in the Banat) in March, although the Gruppe HQ remained near Belgrade.

Ju 87 tug on the airfield at Mostar (Bosnia-Herzegovina) some 150 kms south of Drvar.

Another view of Mostar, with a DFS 230 and Ju 87 tug on the airfield.

A final 'souvenir' photo before boarding the DFS 230. Some 340 SS FJ.Btl.500 men would be landed by glider and tasked with taking six principal objectives. Their departure airfields were located near Zagreb, 170 miles northwest of Drvar.

The transfer of II. and III./LLG 1 to the Balkans is partly explained by the desire to reinforce air transport in territories criss-crossed by partisan bands, by drawing on units that were very inactive (and therefore of little use) in France. The two Gruppen were therefore assigned to XV. Gebirgs-Armeekorps in Croatia. Based in Zirkli and Kraljevo, near Agram, the Ju 87 tugs of II./LLG 1 (Major Eberhard Jahnke) carried out several offensive sorties targeting Bosnian partisans. But since February, German intelligence services had located the headquarters of Josef Brosz, commander of the Yugoslav National Liberation Army, better known as 'Tito', in the Bosnian town of Drvar. An assault using the DFS 230 and paratroopers was conceived – Operation 'Rösselsprung' (a word denoting the movement of the Knight on a chessboard).

For this operation, the planners had the following at their disposal:

* **1. (DFS)/1:** five Schleppzüge (couplings) of Hs 126/DFS 230.
* **2. (DFS)/1:** three Ju 87/DFS 230 sets.
* **II./LLG 1:** eight Ju 87/DFS 230 crews.
* **III./LLG 1:** twelve Hs 126/DFS 230 and five Avia B-534/DFS 230 crews.

In addition, there were about 40 Ju 52s of II./TG 4 available to transport the paratroopers. Most of the 500 or so Fallschirmjäger who reached Drvar by glider or Ju transporter were from the SS-Fallschirmjäger Battalion 500.

The instructions for the raid on 25 May give the distribution of the gliders over the objective:

Preparing the cable on a Henschel HS 126 tug.

1. The command of all parachute and airborne troops is entrusted to SS Hauptsturmführer Kurt Rybka, leading an SS parachute battalion.
2. The paratroopers will be committed in two waves, the first with 340 men, the second with 314 men.
3. The first assault will involve six 'independent' groups:
   * The 'Panther' Kampfgruppe (110 men). Their objective was the seizure of the 'citadel' where Tito and his staff were holed up, according to German intelligence.
   * The 'Greifer' group (40 men). Its task: to capture the British mission.
   * Kampfgruppe 'Stürmer' (50 men) – to capture the Soviet military mission.
   * The 'Brecker' group (50 men) – to capture the American military mission.
   * Kampfgruppe 'Draufgänger' (strength to be determined). Its mission: to capture the 'Westkreuz' sector where Tito's radio station would be located.
   * Kampfgruppe 'Beisser' (20 men). Its mission: to capture an important enemy post and then to assist the 'Greifer' group.
4. The second wave consists of the parachute detachments 'Blau' (110 men), 'Grün' (95 men) and 'Rot' (85 men) which were to capture Drvar and operate in conjunction with the airborne.

The gliders were placed under the command of Lt Hans Sieg of II./LLG 1, who personally led 'Panther' Kampfgruppe, which was responsible for the capture of Tito's headquarters: "During the night of 24-25 May, everything was checked: equipment, weapons, ammunition, etc. The engines of the tugs were run-up and tested. Well before dawn, the men of the SS 500 arrived, waiting to embark. There is a quick pep talk about the flight

SS-Fallschirmjäger prepare to board their DFS 230 early on the morning of 25 May, 1944. Note the addition of a rear-view mirror on the windscreen. There is no machine-gun on the MG mount aft of the cockpit.

and the up-coming combat. At 0555 the take-offs get underway. The landing gear is jettisoned at the end of the runway. We soon see the He 46 and Fiat CR.42 escorts of the Nachtschlachtgruppe 7 and the Croatian Legion.

"Shortly before 0700 we reached the exit of the valley. At 0650 I separate from my tug. I can see Stukas bombing the city and its surroundings. I launch myself into a dive and deploy the braking chute. The heavily loaded glider with its ten occupants brakes in mid-air. The altimeter needle unwinds sharply: 1,500m, 1,000m, 500m... I can see the walls of the citadel and the HQ building. I also notice two flak guns and partisans seeking cover, but I concentrate on the landing. I release the parachute. My speed increases. I touch down and find myself a few metres from the citadel. Machine guns and rifles take us under fire. All the gliders of the 'Panther' group arrived safely except for one whose pilot was hit by defensive fire. The paratroopers quickly exit the glider and go onto the attack..."

The pre-emptive bombardment surprised most of the partisans. Moreover, many of them had never seen paratroopers or gliders before. According to T. Schmiedel: "After the bombing, the partisans come out of their shelters. They see parachutes deploying in the sky. It is some time before the officers order the firing of the guns into this mortal danger. Another spectacle unfolds before their eyes: silent 'birds' falling from the sky. 'Open fire!' an anonymous voice orders. An officer approaches the stationary glider, pulls out his revolver and fires at the machine. A burst from the glider kills him instantly.

"Another glider lands nearby and scrapes the ground with a bang. It has landed near a detachment of partisans who think that the aircraft had come down after being hit by their fire. Coming out of their shelters, they start a victory dance while firing wildly into the air. The ten men in the glider have been thrown forward by the shock of the landing. Now is the critical moment. If the opponent controls his nerves and focuses his fire on the glider, the Landsers have no chance. But here the partisans are laughing and congratulating themselves.

"The glider completes its run-out and comes to a standstill, partially breaking up. The 40 partisans look on in amusement at a wreck. Oberjäger Schutz shouts: 'Out! Get out as fast as you can. Get into position and fire at will!' His comrades extricate themselves from the destroyed machine. It was 7.15am. The enemy has just realised that there are still people in the aircraft. Some of them throw themselves to the ground. Others fire their rifles at the paratroopers. Too late – three FG 42s have

DFS 230s from III./LLG 1 on their way to Drvar towed by Hs 126s.

This Kampfgruppe Panther DFS 230 has come to a stand almost on top of a partisan anti-aircraft position at the edge of the walled cemetery known as the Citadel. Just visible in the background is the Drvar factory area.

The assault proceeds with the Ju 52s overflying the DFS 230 landing zones which became crowded as the different waves of men and material occupied the same small area.

already been deployed and are mowing down the partisans who are now on the defensive…"

Around 12,000 men of the Yugoslav 1st Proletarian Brigade equipped with heavy weaponry defended the sector. The gliders came under heavy fire. As Leutnant Sieg reported, there were casualties shortly before landing. For example, the aircraft of Oblt Friedrich Bredenbeck (11./LLG 1), commanding the 'Greifer' group, was hit by machine-gun fire on its approach, the aircraft hitting the ground some 9km from Drvar. Bredenbeck was killed, as were probably all his passengers.

An Uffz from the 'Draufgänger' group (III./LLG 1) wrote: "We were flying south-east towards Drvar. Shortly before dropping the cable, I noticed Oblt Bredenbeck's glider clearly losing altitude before hitting the ground. It was around 0710. At an altitude of 800m, I spotted the 'Westkreuz' sector. I activated my braking parachute, but it was faulty. I released it. I flew over the target before launching myself further into a 180° turn. I land correctly. My left wing was damaged. The glider had not yet stopped and the SS paratroopers were already disembarking. We got to the nearby houses. I went to the wreckage of the DFS 230 to find some canisters for the flamethrowers. When I came back, I learned that Ogfr. Kielmann had been killed…"

Kielmann seems to have been hit by crossfire after landing his glider, just as he was scrambling clear. Similarly hit by machine-gun fire, Uffz Willi Wicke was severely wounded but managed to drag himself back to his destroyed glider. He died of his wounds the following day. It should be noted that two DFS 230s from II./LLG II carrying ammunition, including 10.5cm shells, could not be unloaded due to the intensity of fire from the partisans.

The aircraft of NSGr 7 then took over the attack. At around 0845, the Germans managed to break

This photo shows the body of a III./LLG 1 pilot, Uffz Kielmann, killed shortly after leaving his glider. Note the MG 34 still strapped to the cockpit.

the main resistance and by 0900 the town had been seized. The attackers had carried out the first part of their plan: to take control of the town. But the bird had already flown. Tito, who was celebrating his 52nd birthday that day, spent most of his time in a cave inside the mountain range surrounding Drvar, for fear of German air attacks. When the parachutists entered the cave, it was empty. The Yugoslav leader had escaped with his staff and their British liaison officer (Major Randolph Churchill) through a tunnel leading to the top of the mountain. With British help, Tito left Yugoslavia, reached Bari and was immediately taken to Vis to set up his new headquarters.

In the meantime, the partisans had received serious reinforcements. As would happen later on the Vercors plateau in France, the surrounded airborne troops met fierce resistance and had to put up a staunch defence. The SS-Fallschirmjäger held out in Drvar until 27 May, when they were rescued by German armoured columns from Bihac and Banja Luka. The defenders had also been supported by Stukas from III./LLG 1.

Five glider pilots were reported to have died during 'Rösselsprung'. In fact there were six: three were shot down during their descent, one (Ogfr Kielmann) was killed shortly after landing and two others (Uffz Reinhard Wenkel and Willi Wicke) were lost in the fighting on the ground. The result of the operation can only be assessed as 'mixed'. Many partisans were captured and a large amount of equipment was seized, but Tito escaped the paratroopers and would continue to lead the Communist resistance until the end of the war after reconstituting his HQ. Having carried out his assignment, Lt Hans Sieg probably merited an award, but, once again, German intelligence had proved to be faulty.

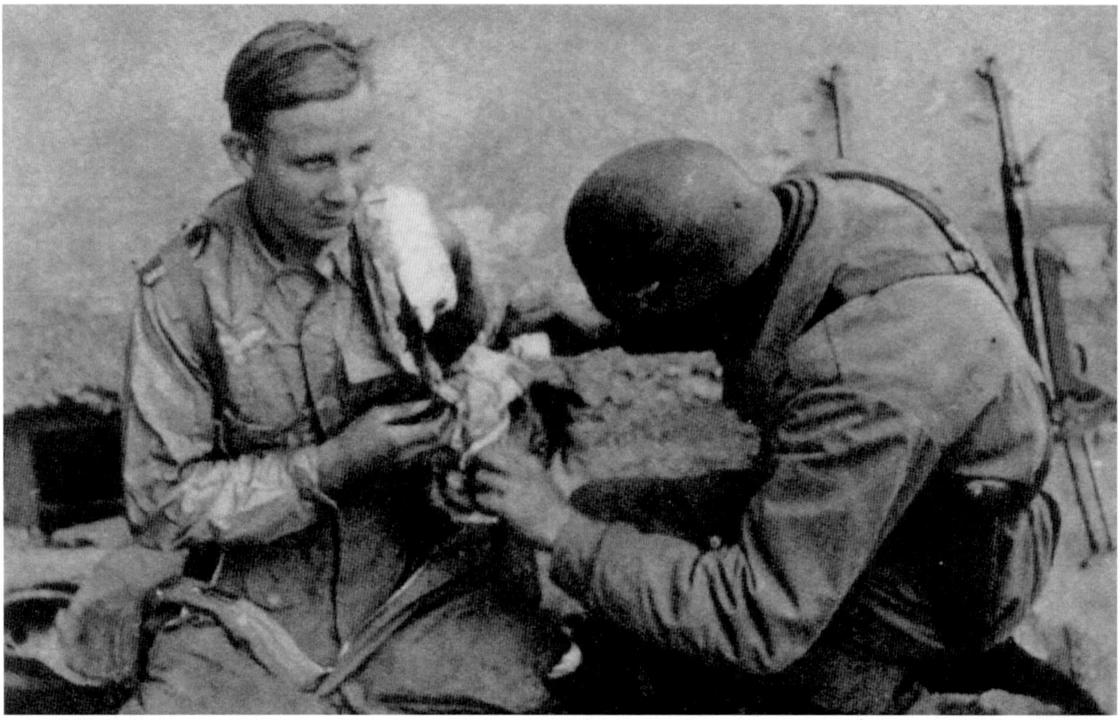

Uffz Willi Wicke (23), wounded by partisans, received first aid from a Fallschirmjäger in the shelter of a building. He was hit again on the night of 25 to 26 May and died a few hours later.

Lt Hans Sieg (KGr 'Panther') takes a breather after the fighting.

Thirteen of the 16 glider pilots of Kampfgruppe 'Panther' photographed shortly after the Drvar battle. They include Uffz Winter (third from right with white helmet), Lt Hans Sieg (sixth from right) and, to Sieg's left, Uffz Batschauer.

At the end of the 1980s, the Yugoslav War Museum (located in Belgrade at the Kalamegdan fortress) exhibited the wreckage of a DFS 230. A Drvar machine or, more probably, one of those abandoned during the German withdrawal of September/October 1944.

1944 / Folge 26 ILLUSTRIERTER BEOBACHTER

Hier saß Josip Broz
Häuser einer kleinen Stadt in den bosnischen Bergen, von der aus der Räuberhauptmann „Tito" (mit wahrem Namen Josip Broz) seine Banditen befehligte. Die Aufnahme wurde von einem amerikanischen Kriegsberichter hergestellt.

DIE „RESIDENZ" DES ZUCHTHÄUSLERS

SS-FALLSCHIRMJÄGER SPRINGEN INS ZENTRUM DER BANDENGRUPPEN DES JOSIP BROZ

Vor kurzem meldete der Wehrmachtbericht die Zerschlagung des Zentrums der Bandengruppen des Zuchthäuslers Josip Broz. In schweren Kämpfen, bei denen sich die 7. SS-Gebirgsdivision „Prinz Eugen" und das

Eine Aktion deutscher SS-Fallschirmjäger beginnt.
Die dritte und vierte Kette springt, während die schon gelandeten SS-Fallschirmjäger sich zum Angriff sammeln.

Rechts: Wieder sind einige Häuser von Banditen gesäubert.

Am zweiten Tag: Das Unternehmen wird durchgeführt.

"SS-paras jump into the lair of the Josip Broz terrorist group. Tito's bandits smashed in Wehrmachtbericht report" — *Illustrierter Beobachter* newspaper article from late June 1944.

11

VERCORS – WITH KG 200 AGAINST THE FRENCH RESISTANCE

ASSEMBLED IN the now German sector of Alsace/Lorraine, LLGs 1 and 2 largely abandoned French soil. In February 1944, III./LLG 1 left Nancy for Serbia, settling in Alibunar and then Krusevac. Shortly afterwards, II./LLG 1 left for Zagreb (Croatia).

By this time, there was no longer any doubt that an Allied landing in France was imminent. To reinforce the coastal sector if necessary, Operation 'Sporturlaub' (Sporting Leave!) was launched. I./LLG 1 (Hauptmann Krug) based at Strasbourg-Entzheim began night landing exercises using flares, with the aim of supplying German troops facing the landing forces. The first test took place in Strasbourg on the evening of May 9, 1944 – four years to the day after the operation targeting Ében-Émael and the bridges on the Albert Canal. The trials seemed to have been conclusive, but the following month the fighting in Normandy was such that gliders could not be used in this way.

Glider units in France were thus reduced to just I./LLG 1 and 1./LLG 2. A few crews from these two units were then deployed in the south of France against 'partisans'. For months, the Vercors mountain range had been home to a large group of Maquis that had benefited from Allied parachute drops as well as advisers from British SOE and the American OSS. A few clashes took place as early as January 1944, with the 'maquisards' already supplied with weapons. The Normandy landings on 6 June only exacerbated the situation. On 14 July, a major airdrop of weapons, ammunition and equipment was organised by the USAAF, which could only strengthen the Maquis.

Opposite them, the Germans had painstakingly assembled a very disparate force with the aim of eradicating this well-structured group of resistance fighters. Fighter-bombers and captured aircraft had been operating since 24 June, but there were not enough of them and they were not powerful enough to weaken the enemy, but by 21 July the Germans felt strong enough to launch Operation 'Bettina' – four Kampfgruppen (combat groups) were to attack the Vercors in four different locations, while a large detachment of airborne troops was to be dropped by glider near the village of Vassieux, one of the strong points of the Maquis.

A few days earlier, around 20 Do 17s from I./LLG 1 towing DFS 230s had arrived at Lyon-Bron. The future passengers were parachutists operating under the cover name 'Transportkolonne XI-Ost' initially assembled in Dedelstorf under a Major

Jungwirt in October 1943. They were subsequently trained for a 'Sondereinsatz' and were held in reserve to deploy as an air assault unit of around 350 men on missions to be undertaken by Kampfgeschwader 200, a top-secret 'special ops' unit which operated in close collaboration with the Abwehr.

At dawn on 21 July, the bombers towed their gliders into the air and headed for the Vercors. One Staffel (reduced to seven or eight gliders) was planned to land near the hamlets of Weiler le Château and La Mure, the other in Vassieux itself. The formation initially followed the Rhône valley. Near Valence, it turned eastwards then northwards. One glider, victim of a broken cable, was forced to carry out an emergency landing. After an hour and a half flying time, the gliders separated from the Dorniers. At that time, they were about 10km from their objective and at an altitude of 2,500m.

The pilots commenced their diving approach, braking parachutes were deployed and nose rockets were fired. Although the rockets failed to work in two of the gliders, their pilots still managed to land them without much difficulty. The attack on the hamlets was a success. Benefiting from the effect of surprise, the airborne troops put the resistance fighters present out of action (around 20 civilians were also killed in this action). Then, the airborne force (pilots included) barricaded themselves in the houses transformed into strongholds.

In Vassieux, the effect of surprise was not so great and two DFS 230s were destroyed. The aircraft flown by Uffz Eberhardt Pyritz hit a house while Uffz Friedrich Rink's machine smashed into a rocky outcrop near the landing strip. Their occupants were all killed. Pilot Siegfried Kurre was luckier. His glider crashed to the ground after flying into a high-tension cable. The pilot and his crew were unhurt. The evacuation of the other gliders was carried out in order, but under heavy fire from the resistance fighters. The Germans nevertheless took the village hard but, like their comrades a little further north, found themselves surrounded by the FFI (French Forces of the Interior – the resistance) who were far superior in number. Several unsuccessful attacks were launched by the French while the Luftwaffe tried to weaken the enemy with sporadic bombings.

The next day, 22 July, 1944, a second planned arrival of airborne troops had to be aborted due to bad weather, although a few aircraft managed to drop supply containers at Vassieux. Around 20 other glider teams from I./LLG 1 as well as two Gothas from I./LLG 2 had arrived shortly beforehand at the Valence-Chabeuil aerodrome and were due to take on board around 50 paratroopers but also Ostlegionnäre, volunteers from the east, as well as heavy equipment. On the 23rd, the gliders were able to take off but, close to the plateau, the formation encountered violent winds and two DFS 230s had to crash land at Marignac-en-Diois and the Col d'Ancise after their tow cables snapped. A third (piloted by Uffz August Birzer) had a wing torn off and crashed at Montjoux. On the plateau, there were more losses. One of the Go 242s landed correctly in the perimeter held by the Germans but a second landed too far away for its cargo to be recovered. One of the DFS 230s of I./LLG 1 (piloted by Uffz Hermann Metzen) hit an obstacle and disintegrated, killing several of its occupants including the pilot.

The airborne seemed at this time to have been able to widely extend their defence perimeter, thus allowing the landing of Fi 156s near Vassieux to evacuate the wounded. Finally, on the 24th, a Go 242 brought in a 20mm flak cannon whose powerful fire sounded the death knell for the encirclement of Vassieux.

For their part, the land Kampfgruppen were able to progress before joining up. On 25 July, the maquis were considered to have been eliminated. According to an LLG 1 pilot: "In the early morning of 25 July, the bulk of the paratroopers and the glider pilots were going to head towards

Grenoble … Given the stifling heat and dust, we covered our dead with tents. We first loaded them into a Fi 156 before clearing a temporary track by removing as many rocks and other obstacles as possible. Two Ju 52s landed without difficulty in the afternoon. The rest of the bodies were loaded into one of them and we climbed into the second which took us to Lyon…"

Operation 'Bettina' resulted in the deaths of some 570 resistance fighters but also 131 civilians. Sixty-five German soldiers were reported killed and 18 others missing. Among the victims, there were four glider pilots who – since the Eastern Front—were no longer simple 'transport aviators' but front-line combatants like their passengers. Some 43 DFS 230s and three Go 242s took part in the operation and those that had brought in troops were abandoned on the plateau and set on fire.

Gefallen! Diese Schreckenskunde.
Schlug unsern Herzen tiefe Wunden.
Gram und Schmerz will uns verzehren.
Denn niemals wird er wiederkehren.
Er, der so lieb war und so gut.
Hingeben mußte er sein teures Blut.
Du hast uns ja so oft geschrieben:
Macht keine Sorgen Euch, Ihr Lieben,
Ich kehr' zurück, auf Wiedersehen!

Schwer und für uns noch unfaßbar traf uns die Nachricht, daß unser über alles geliebter Sohn, Bruder und Bräutigam

Hermann Metzen

Flugzeugführer
in einer Segelflugstaffel

am 23. Juli 1944 bei La Mur (Südfrankreich) mit seinem Flugzeug tödlich abgestürzt ist.

Der liebe Verstorbene war geboren am 17. Dezember 1921. Der Tod trifft die Eltern besonders hart, denn für sie gab er sein Letztes hin.

„Ruhe Dich aus, geliebter Hermann, wir sehen uns wieder."

Um ihn trauern seine schmerzgeprüften Eltern, seine Brüder Josef und Theo, seine geliebte Braut Liselotte sowie alle Anverwandten.

I/0216

Death card for a DFS pilot Hermann Menzen killed during 'Bettina'.

DFS 230 getting airborne behind a Do 17 somewhere in the south of France.

DFS 230 of LLG 1 landed at Vassieux in the Vercors.

DFS 230 which crashed at the Col d'Ancise (Coll. Chapus).

12

ONE-WAY FLIGHTS TO HELL – BUDAPEST, BRESLAU AND BERLIN

According to the military adage: "Old soldiers never die, they just fade away". Such was the fate of the DFS 230 gliders of the Luftwaffe...

At the beginning of 1945, of all the glider units that had succeeded each other in the Luftwaffe, only one 'official' Staffel had escaped a general dissolution order promulgated during September 1944: 2./LLG 1 renamed 'Schleppstaffel z.b.V. Reich' (z.b.V. – zur besonderen Verwendung or 'special purpose'). Based at Altenstadt, it comprised 18 Do 17s and the same number of DFS 230s.

For its part, Schleppgruppe 1, which had returned from the Balkans with difficulty, was more or less active with a few Go 242s (probably based at Sagan) and DFS 230s. The other gliders scattered in the rest of the Reich were effectively 'grounded', stoically awaiting their fate – the 'coup de grace' from Allied fighter-bombers bludgeoning their airfields on a daily basis or being blown-up as ground troops approached.

BUDAPEST

On 1 January 1945, however, an officer of the Staffel z.b.V. Reich was urgently called to Berlin to learn that the 70,000 or so German and Hungarian soldiers encircled in Budapest had to be supplied by air as soon as possible. This could only be done with DFS 230s and, after a discussion held in Papa on 6 January, a 'landing strip' was prepared on a grassy area in the heart of Budapest. About 50m wide and 150m long, this 'meadow' (the so-called 'Blutwiese' or 'blood meadow' in Buda on the left bank of the Danube) would allow Fi 156 Storks to land to pick up the pilots.

On 17 January, a dozen DFS 230s arrived at Papa with some eight Ju 87s. That same day, Ofhr Rolf Mütter took off shortly before midnight with a glider loaded with a ton of ammunition and mail. He could not release the wheels (which could be dangerous on landing). Near the Hungarian capital, he separated from his tug and dived towards the landing site after opening his parachute. Luckily, the undercarriage broke away on impact with the ground and, as the braking rockets fired properly, the DFS 230 stopped its slide in a matter of metres.

However, Mütter was not immediately welcomed by his fellow countrymen because the flames from the rockets made it look like a crash. Eventually the pilot was rescued and brought before the Commander-in-Chief of Defence, SS

DFS 230 wrecked during a bombing raid on Hildesheim.

Obergruppenführer Karl Pfeffer von Wildenbruch, who congratulated him warmly on his daring. Rolf Mütter was luckier than the pilot of another glider who had left at the same time but hurriedly put down after being hit by enemy flak.

The next day, on the 18th, six gliders failed to land in Budapest, three being lost with their pilots.

On the night of 20/21 January, 20 DFS 230 gliders were launched for Budapest, 17 reached their destination. Given the limited number of aircraft available, Hptm Klaus-Dieter Reich (Staka of the z.b.V. Reich) personally ensured four of these tows into the burning city. One of the gliders, flown by Ogfr Schlüpmann, was one of the few machines of Schleppgruppe 1. Schlüpmann dropped his cable over Budapest but orbited the city for a while without being able to locate the landing site. Forced to land in enemy territory, he was captured while trying to return to his lines.

On 23 January, of the 11 gliders that were sent to Budapest, seven released their tow cables, of which only four managed to put down in German-held territory. Uffz Jäger described his flight into Budapest: "It is the evening of 23 January 1945 on the airfield at Papa. Dusk is setting in and with it the bitter cold. The sudden drop in temperature causes ground fog to form. The gliders are readied to get airborne while the Do 17 and He 111 tugs run up their engines. Everyone runs around freezing and in a state of tension. The cigarettes from the pre-sortie meal are smoked even though smoking is not allowed. "2215 Uhr Start frei" – take offs from 2215. My Do 17 tug swirls up the snow and disappears from view. The DFS 230 glider starts to roll, becomes airborne and chases after the invisible Dornier. Just the exhaust flames and position lights are visible.

"Imperceptibly the tug climbs, safety height is 2,000m. Slowly, the grim cold seeps through my boots and flight suit. The phosphorescent instruments in front of me glow brightly and interfere with my night vision. The Dornier continues to climb into the frosty sky. Over Stuhlweissenburg we get the first anti-aircraft fire, the shell bursts causing the characteristic bucking. To be on the safe side we climb a little higher and are out of range at 3,000m. All around muzzle flashes mark out the position of the frontlines. After some 40 minutes in the air I catch sight of the white ribbon of the Danube, now seemingly icebound after the recent freezing nights. Just a little further and the twin-city on the river should come into view.

"When we reach the Danube, we make a left turn, now using the river as a signpost to fly towards Budapest. The searchlights have taken up their work and are scanning the frosty sky. After exactly one hour's flight, I recognise a huge dark spot stretching out on both sides of the Danube – Budapest! As my altitude is sufficient I pull the release lever and separate from the tug. Below me I can make out the first of the seven Danube bridges. There are red fires blazing, marking the location of heavy fighting. Now and then the beam from a searchlight sweeps past, lighting up the cockpit.

"The altimeter shows 3,000m as I arrive over the city. Suddenly I'm caught in a terrible cone of light. I fly a steep turn to the left, control stick hard over and it is not long before I am in darkness again. The bitter cold leaves no feeling at all in my feet and hands. Slowly as my altitude decreases the outlines of several housing blocks come into focus. At 2,000m I fly around Buda once more. I can see nothing of the supposedly existing flashing lights and light signals! In the south of the city, a white flare is suddenly fired, followed by others.

"My altitude is sufficient for a ditching there, although the landing strip cannot possibly be there according to the pre-sortie briefing. Also, the indication on my map does not correspond with the spot I have just marked with a flare. The firing of flares stops and a strip is lit up intermittently like a beacon. As I fly back over the edge of the city, I clearly recognise the spot marked by the Russians as a decoy landing strip – a trap... there are no houses bordering it and no sign of the DFS 230s that took off ahead of me. With the height I had left I had still to find the actual strip. Once again, I head back over the city. The outlines of houses and streets grow clearer. Should I put down in one of these roads? That would be my last option.

"I have the map in my hand and the full moon lights up the cockpit. The strip must be below me. I'm at 400m altitude. I circle again, throwing open the side plexiglass panel so I can see better. Suddenly I spot three small white lights. Finally, I have an indication of our landing strip. Now to attempt the difficult part of the flight – the landing. Along a road we head towards the landing lights. The last houses are approaching, but I still have plenty of height. Landing flaps deployed, side slip down. The aircraft starts to shudder under the stresses. I end the sideslip, line up correctly. The ground is rapidly approaching. I fly over the house. Now to put down quickly, because who knows how long the strip is. I hold the control stick back into my stomach and the glider rears up and sinks like a stone. I hit the ground hard and the glider slips and slides and slides.

"Ahead of me to the left a dark spot, and to the right I can see other gliders. One brief moment and there's a crashing and splintering all around me. The fright is quickly over and when everything remains calm I clamber out of the cockpit. Now I really notice the cold, because there's no feeling in my feet. I trudge off helplessly and slowly take in my surroundings. I look at my DFS 230. There's not much of it left that is recognisable as an aircraft – port wing torn off, starboard wing just a stub and the tailplane missing..."

Bad weather continued to hamper glider flights into the city. On the night of 4 to 5 February, of the five DFS 230s sent out, only two reached their destination.

On 11 February, the garrison still present in

The particularly risky nature of night landings in Budapest is confirmed by the fate of this DFS 230 H4-2-6 of the Staffel z.b.V. Reich which crashed into a building in József Attila Str. Note the distinctive mark (a circle?) painted on the tail plane.

This accident is said to have taken place on 4 February 1945 and the name of the pilot is given as Georg-Adolf Schmall from Berlin. However, he is not on the list of those who disappeared in Budapest and, according to another source, the pilot was Ofw Georg Filius (killed on 30 January 1945).

Budapest surrendered. Some 73 DFS 230s were involved in the resupply sorties, with 41 machines able to carry out their assigned mission. Eleven gliders fell victim to flak or were forced to land outside the zone held by German-Hungarian troops. Forty-nine pilots were reported missing. Only a small minority were able to return from the Soviet camps years later.

BRESLAU

No sooner had Budapest surrendered than the surviving DFS 230 gliders were deployed in support of the encircled city of Breslau, a 'Festung' or 'fortress' way behind Russian lines and which the Russians were determined to occupy (today Wroclaw). Some 45,000 German troops and 250,000 civilians were trapped there. On 16 February, Ju 52s and He 111s were called up from all four corners of a shrinking Reich to mount resupply operations into the city but as these aircraft had suffered heavy losses, gliders had to be used. For sorties into Breslau the remnants of Schleppgruppe 1 were more or less reestablished, with Staffel z.b.V. Reich arriving from Papa at the end of February with 11 Do 17s and some 25 DFS 230s to become 4./Schleppgruppe 1.

Despite the organisational chaos reigning just about everywhere in the Reich at that stage of the war, by 27 February 1945 some 228 DFS 230 gliders and a similar number of aircrew had been assembled (alongside large numbers of Gotha Go 242s) from bases all over Germany to operate under the Transportfliegerführer Luftflotte 6 out of Hohenmauth in Bohemia-Moravia, north-east of Prague.

Uffz Wilhelm Itter (who had taken part in the fighting at Vercors) was captured in Budapest on 23 January 1945. Note the circle painted on the tail plane.

Wrecks of DFS 230s littering the grassy expanse of Budapest's improvised airfield.

By now Breslau was the focus of a large-scale battle. The Russians were bent on disrupting air transport activity by building up anti-aircraft and searchlight batteries, concentrated particularly towards the airfield east of the city, Gandau. As this airfield soon came under Soviet artillery fire, the city authorities had urgently sought to build an ad-hoc strip within the city by widening the main thoroughfare, Kaiser Straße. Although never used by motorised transports due to the fires and pall of smoke hanging almost permanently over the city, the DFS 230 pilots were able to put down on it. Forced to carry out their flights at night and in appalling weather conditions, including sudden dense fog, the DFS 230s brought in a battalion of paratroopers to support the garrison even before work on the strip was completed in late February. Picked up by searchlights as they glided in, the DFS 230s were subject to heavy fire, and landings, according to Morzik's account, "were made under the most trying conditions imaginable..."

Georg Schlaug detailed one particular mission: "On the evening of 22 March 1945, on Hitler's personal orders, six heavy guns with their crews and ammunition were to be transported to the Breslau Festung. Three Go 242s piloted by Fw Frohn, Ofw Seidel and Ofw Huber and three DFS 230s took off at night. These first operations proved just how gruelling and costly the flights to Breslau would be. Fw Frohn hit an obstacle when his glider landed in Kaiserstraße. Ofw Seidel's Gotha was caught in searchlight beams as it dropped its cable and was hit by flak. It was able to put down quickly, but landed behind Soviet lines. It took the pilot and three gunners seven days to reach the fortress. Only Ofw Huber was able to land correctly.

Likewise, the sorties of the three DFS 230s were chaotic and confused. One machine had to return due to technical problems. The second crashed near Grossenheim, with pilot Walter Krause seriously injured. The third DFS crashed on the southern edge of the fortress, killing its pilot, Uffz Walter Helsinger. On the following nights, a Go 242 had to return due to lack of visibility. On the night of 26/27 March, a DFS piloted by Uffz Hustert was able to land in the fortress..."

During the first ten days of April, 29 gliders were committed, but only 10 of them reached Breslau. Every flight involved a feat of airmanship and a potential 'adventure' on the ground. On the evening of 7 April, Uffz Rolf Singenstreu was separated from his tug too early and his DFS 230 landed in Soviet territory on one of the banks of the Oder. Hiding by day and moving only at night, the pilot followed the river towards Breslau. On the night of the 10th, he found a boat and covered the last most dangerous part of the journey into the fortress on the water, taking advantage of the distraction of Soviet sentries watching flak fire aimed at a He 111 that had come to drop containers on the city to jump in and swim to the German 'side'.

On 23 April, he was evacuated by Fi 156 from the fortress. His Staffel comrade, Uffz Stephan, flew into the city a few nights later: "Breslau was my home town, so naturally I volunteered to fly the sortie in Hptm Reich's Staffel, at that time based in Alt-Lönnewitz. We were given reconnaissance photos of the city to study in preparation, including images taken at night in clear conditions, similar to those under which these sorties would be flown. The fires and the notable river network of Breslau were clearly visible, which would be a useful navigation aid at altitude.

"The landing strip lighting would only be visible from around 1,000-1,500m. We knew that the Russians were using decoy landing lights on their territory to mislead us, so orientation by the landing lights alone could easily lead us straight into Russian hands. The heavy losses to date were mainly attributed to artillery fire during landing and our aircraft being shot down when flying back out of the city, among other things. Our tugs were Do 17s and He 111s. Like many of the other pilots I had not previously been towed by either of these machines. Not only that, but my last night flight had taken place more than one year previously.

"During April – with the front approaching Alt-Lönnewitz on both sides – Schleppgruppe 1 moved to Hohenmauth in the then Protectorate (Bohemia-Moravia). I made the transfer to Hohenmauth behind a He 111 at first light, flying my heavily laden DFS at very low level to avoid the large numbers of enemy fighters. My flight into Breslau took place as night was falling. The tug pilot was Staffelkapitän Reich himself. The distance to cover to Breslau was about 140km... The take off and approach were free of incident and communication with the tug via the throat microphone worked perfectly. The night was starry and clear and long before the release I could see the huge fires lighting up the sky ahead of us.

"Around 20km from Breslau and at a height of 3,500-4,000m I received the instruction from the tug pilot to prepare for separation. He hurriedly gave me the information about our position, course and altitude. It was then that the first searchlights flashed on... ich klinkte aus... I released the tow cable and maintained course towards the fires. For a while I was captivated by the grandiose sight of the burning city, its fires illuminating huge clouds of smoke up to great heights. I had almost overlooked the fact that the probing beams of the searchlights were getting closer and closer.

"Suddenly my cockpit was lit up brightly. They had spotted me. Instinctively I pulled up into a tight turn and soon I was enveloped in reassuring darkness. I modified my heading, now flying towards the East. The searchlight beams remained behind me. At this altitude I could afford a diversion and then approach the fortress from the south-east, following the course of the Oder river. The advantage of this was that I avoided the reflection of the fires in the north-western harbour district of the city and was also not forced to 'fly

Unser lieber Sohn, Bruder und Neffe
Feldwebel
Ernst Huber,
gab bei einem Versorgungsflug
am 10. April 1945 sein Leben
im Alter von 27 Jahren.
R. I. P.

Du lebst im Herzen Deiner Lieben,
Du bist nur ferne, bist nicht tot;
Dir ist dort leuchtend aufgegangen
Des wahren Lebens Morgenrot.

Although a report states that Fw Ernst Huber of Schl. Gr. 1 landed safely in Breslau, his 'death card' records that he died on 10 April during a resupply operation into the encircled city of Breslau. According to one source, he was killed on the railway tracks at Breslau station. Note that he wore glasses, which was rare for flying personnel.

blind' in the clouds of smoke. I arrived over the city at around 1,000m and soon spotted the landing lights on the field strip. I could also see the clearly identifiable flashes as artillery shells impacted the field and the Kaiserstrasse. To the north of the town there was a Russian landing strip – clearly lit up – but too far away from the flood channel to tempt me to land. I knew that I was coming down on the landing strip along the flood channel. I accepted the disadvantage of having to come in along the tree-lined dyke. In almost textbook fashion I spiralled down to lose height.

"Unfortunately, on the last curve, the shadow of a large house interfered with my landing preparations. I veered off course to avoid it but my speed was much too fast. The trees along the dyke were far beneath me and the red lamp at the end of the strip was disconcertingly close – and rapidly drawing closer! When I saw the shadow of the bridge coming towards me—as a Breslau native I knew that it rested on huge stone pillars – I kept the glider in the sideslip and let it hit the ground at an angle. The barbed wire around the skid quickly brought it to a stand. My head was banged violently against the metal frame of the canopy but fortunately, when releasing the cable, I had put on my steel FJ helmet ('Springerhelm').

"Largely undamaged, the machine had come to a stand, just metres from the bridge structure and the water. A vehicle drove out towards me. Men with axes and other tools jumped down to greet me with hugs and set about recovering the glider cargo. Although still dazed I was taken to a nearby Gefechtsstand and given a glass of Schnapps, while my glider was dismantled, chopped into pieces and thrown into the river. The Russians would discover no trace of a landing."

Uffz Stephan had enjoyed better fortune than a comrade who had followed him down, misjudged his landing attempt and crashed, ploughing into the tops of the trees. The cockpit was wrecked and the pilot badly injured. Both Stephan and the injured pilot were flown out of Breslau in a Fi 156 Storch towards the end of April.

Throughout April, the glider units (like the rest of the Luftwaffe) had to cope not only with losses but also with fuel shortages. Added to this were the bombings by the Allied air force, which destroyed tugs and gliders on the airfields.

On the night of 29/30 April, the last sortie into

the city was flown by four DFS 230s (Uffz Kutzas, Fw Becker, Fw Krösche and Uffz Thies). Three of them reached the besieged city.

According to Schlaug, at least two pilots (Uffz Kutzas and Hustert) flew two missions to Breslau (being flown back after the first). In mid-April, a Ju 52 leaving the fortress was shot down as it was bringing back several Lastensegler pilots. Among the names of the missing was that of Fw Fritz Haupt, a DFS 230 pilot who had taken part in the Corinth and Crete operations.

On 8 May 1945, the order came to scuttle gliders and tow planes. This was followed by the forced march west to surrender to the Western Allies. But many members of Schleppgruppe 1 were handed over by the US Army to the Soviets.

BERLIN

By late April 1945 Germany had effectively been cut in two and German-held territory was shrinking rapidly. The last airfield within the city limits of Berlin was Gatow and on April 27, 1945, Gatow was overrun by the Russians. With this loss, Berlin's last airfield for heavy aircraft, few Luftwaffe aircraft were still able to fly into the city. The defenders' only hope for any further operations was the Charlottenburger Chaussee (the so-called 'Ost-West Achse'), designated as a takeoff and landing strip by Hitler in his 'order for the preparations of the defence of the Reichs capital'. The 'east-west axis' was a wide and long boulevard in central Berlin but no large multi-engined aircraft could hope to land here. It could be used as an ad-hoc landing ground by smaller aircraft. So, operating from a handful of airfields on the Baltic coast and hauled by TGr. 30 He 111 Schleppmaschine (tugs), some of the Luftwaffe's most futile, desperate and final flights were flown by DFS 230 gliders and their young pilots into the doomed Reichshauptstadt Berlin.

Only a matter of weeks before the end, Major Walter Hornung, Transportfliegerführer Luftflotte Reich, ordered the establishment of an ad hoc Schleppstaffel for glider operations into Berlin. This tug unit was thrown together from Heinkel He 111s parked at airfields in northern Germany and equipped with towing gear. A 'new' 4./TGr. 30 under Hptm Matthies, a former Staffelkapitän in LLG 1, operating alongside a 'strengthened' 3./TGr. 30, formed the so-called 'Einsatzgruppe Uhl'under Maj. Fritz Uhl. The DFS 230s of this unit arrived by road at Tarnewitz in the last week of April 1945. Here they were assembled and flown to Rerik and Großenbrode (north-east of Hamburg). DFS pilot Fw Helmut Witte had flown into Berlin on 26 April to organise the unloading of gliders arriving in the city and the return of the pilots to their bases, but the chaotic situation at Gatow – which was under heavy Soviet artillery fire – saw him fly out in a Storch and back to Rerik almost immediately. Despite this, Hornung's plan to use DFS 230 gliders to 'supply' Berlin was not abandoned – quite the opposite.

With the loss of Flughafen Gatow, the main resupply effort – flown by Heinkel He 111s of II./KG 4 – was the dropping of supply canisters at low level. According to 'Kampfkommandant Berlin' General Weidling's report, on the night of 28-29 April some six tons of supplies had been delivered into the city in this way – "in other words, virtually nothing". Urgent radio messages were still being transmitted from Hitler's bunker for outside help. During the afternoon of 27 April 1945 an insistent call reached Dönitz's HQ in northern Germany – a landing attempt had to be made on the East-West Axis with all available means.

On the night of 28-29 April, five DFS 230s took off from Rerik on the Baltic sea coast with Uffz Kestner, Uffz Schleicher, Uffz Kugler, Ogfr Heine and Gefr Heim at their controls. The east-west axis ('Ost-West Achse') was swept by heavy artillery fire and no landings were attempted. Uffz Kugler took advantage of the fires burning in the centre to locate a large flat area and carried out a landing in the district of Tegel. His cargo of anti-aircraft shells was immediately recovered and used by a nearby flak battery.

Heinkel He 111 tugs and crew of the so-called 'Einsatzgruppe Uhl' seen here on 1 May 1945 in Großenbrode (north-east of Hamburg). Note the mottled finish on the He 111 WNr 4226. VIA PAUL STIPDONK

DFS 230s abandoned at an airfield in 1945.

Kugler, like his comrades, was carrying an authorisation of safe passage which allowed him to climb into one of the last aircraft leaving the area and return to Rerik. Although he was wounded in the head, he survived the war but did not mention in his account the 'airfield' or the aircraft involved. The fate of the other pilots is unknown – with one exception. Gfr. Heim was forced to make an emergency landing before reaching Berlin, probably due to engine failure of the He 111 that was towing him. As Hptm Matthies was reported killed on a towing flight on the same night it is likely that he was the tug pilot.

At Tarnewitz the following afternoon, 29 April, a Fw Heinz Schäfer witnessed two DFS 230 gliders getting airborne. These gliders had arrived the previous evening departing Rostock Marienehe to Tarnewitz towed by a Heinkel He 111 of 3./TGr. 30. Schäfer told author Georg Schlaug that the glider pilots' Einsatzbefehle (mission orders) included the instruction; "Gruppe bereithalten, Führer aus Berlin zu befreien" – 'stand ready to fly Hitler out of Berlin'. Which indicates of course that one aim of these last desperate attempts to reach central Berlin was to prolong for a short while longer the lives of those in the bunker – including that of Adolf Hitler – so that a possible attempt might be made to fly him out to 'safety'.

On the night of 29-30 April (or 30 April-1 May?), two more DFS 230s flew to Berlin. Wilhelm Schneider's machine was hit by flak and its pilot, seriously wounded, landed near the east-west axis and was immediately captured by the Soviets. The pilot of the other glider, Uffz Göbel, was killed attempting a landing...

It is not known how many DFS 230s flew into Berlin during the last week of April 1945 – possibly as many as 40. Those glider pilots still in Rerik went into British captivity. The DFS 230 had flown its last sortie. Gliders for transport and combat had had their day. Post-war these roles would be filled by helicopters.

AFTERWORD

As author Jean-Louis Roba has explained: "More than seven decades since the end of the Second World War, the accepted view is that the German air force of the Third Reich was a large powerful force with sophisticated aircraft and fanatical fighters. No one seems to question the real value of an air force that ceased to exist in 1919 following the restrictions of the Treaty of Versailles and endured a long hiatus of 15 years (1919-1934) that effectively wiped out the development of military aviation in Germany. While, within just five years, the Luftwaffe enjoyed remarkable growth, it remained extremely fragile.

"The creation of 'conventional' fighter and bomber units took precedence, and the lack of resources (and raw materials) meant that a multitude of projects had to be shelved; for example, the Luftwaffe never had a strategic bomber of value. Transport was also one of the poor relations of the fledgling Luftwaffe, the force having to make do with the trimotor Ju 52 – itself a militarised civilian aircraft. Despite the so-called 'Blitzkrieg', despite early victories, the Luftwaffe was unable to fight effectively over a long period (let alone on several fronts) with units shuttled backwards and forwards constantly..."

The glider arm of the Luftwaffe illustrates the above perfectly. The DFS 230, praised and flown by Ernst Udet, was an aircraft that had no real role in the pre-war Luftwaffe. A few were built, but had attracted only a few committed supporters. However, aware of the shortage of transport aircraft, General Student hit upon the idea of attaching a Staffel of DFS 230s to his 7. Fliegerdivision in 1938 and production of the DFS 230 was relaunched. Then came the Albert Canal operation, which threw the DFS 230 into the propaganda spotlight in May 1940, giving it exaggerated importance.

Subsequent campaigns were to prove somewhat disappointing for the DFS 230, with mixed successes at Corinth and Crete, followed by the obvious failure at Ösel. With the paras having sustained heavy losses those remaining troops were downgraded to 'elite' infantrymen and the DFS 230 gliders reverted to their original role, that of transporters carrying supplies to Wehrmacht units scattered across the vast expanses of the new Eastern Front and the sands of the African desert.

Throughout the five years or so of the war, the DFS 230 saw service on all fronts and its Staffeln underwent regular reorganisation, at times being attached to the Transportgeschwader and at times operating independently with their tugs. Regularly split up and dispersed according to the needs of the front, dispatched to far-flung locations before being recalled –Stalingrad was a good example – this seemingly anarchic management betrayed the lack of cohesion and resources within the Luftwaffe. The need for gliders capable of carrying heavier loads led to the introduction of even bigger gliders – the Go 242 and Me 321 in 1941. These were then motorised (Go 244, Me 323) with all the shortcomings that these hastily conceived projects and concepts entailed.

The DFS 230 survived the entire war, being deployed and flying what amounted to combat sorties right up to the capitulation of the Reich. The glider crews (and those of the transport units) did not of course enjoy the notoriety of the fighter or even the bomber pilots, made famous by the propaganda services but it would be a mistake to think of them as no more than 'drivers', transporting supplies from airfield to airfield. The reality was on occasion somewhat different. The DFS 230 was a fighting aircraft, capable – in modern parlance – of bringing 'shock and awe' and landing soldiers directly into the combat zone, something which was even attempted in North Africa. All of which was rather different from the Allied approach to the deployment of gliders.

While, during the attack on the Albert Canal, the DFS 230 pilots were not necessarily committed as part of the ground forces, later on during the war the glider crews had to be ready to make the 'ultimate sacrifice', especially when flying into the many different 'pockets' in the East. Whether at Kholm, Velikié Louki, Breslau, Budapest or in the Kuban, the glider pilots risked fighter and flak attacks en route to unprepared, inadequate landing strips, even having to put down on fields and roads.

The pilots, aware of the importance of these flights for the encircled troops, accepted quasi-suicidal missions – dubbed 'Himmelfahrtkommandos'. Bringing ammunition, weapons, food, medicine and also mail, they would knowingly tie their fate to that of the besieged troops, knowing full well that the chances of being picked up by a Fi 156 or Ju 52 were uncertain. All of these operations were, in the words of Morzik, "...desperate last resorts. Viewed objectively they had no justification – there was no chance of preventing the capitulation of a city by the employment of air transport units." Despite this, there was never a shortage of volunteers for these very high-risk missions, and the large number of glider crews reported missing is proof of their courage and determination. But there was also a more sinister aspect. The glider pilots were an 'elite'; some of their number were ideologically 'radicalised' and both volunteered for and dreamt up all sorts of hare-brained schemes.

Wilhelm Fulda volunteered for the ramming unit Sonderkommando Elbe that flew a single mission against a USAF bombing raid on 7 April 1945. Wounded at Ében-Émael and on Crete, Karl-Heinz Lange is now recognised as the 'brains' behind the so-called Sonderstaffel Einhorn, a unit set up in late 1944, that was – echoing his first combat mission – to specialise in pin-point attacks on bridges. But not as at the Albert Canal by diving on them at the controls of a DFS 230 – but as 'kamikazes' in Fw 190s laden with explosives.

THE DFS 331

The DFS 331 was a cargo glider developed in collaboration between DFS and Gotha. The glider was designed by Jacobs and his design addressed many of the shortcomings present in the DFS 230. The visibility from the cockpit was good, with the entire nose being glazed, and the body was very wide, allowing it to carry light Flak guns and light military vehicles. Contrary to what can be read elsewhere only a single example was constructed which flew for the first time on 30 September 1940. Although the aircraft was flown and tested ahead of the Go 242, development on the type was halted by the RLM in March 1941.

Oblt Karl-Heinz Blendermann, Staffelführer of 2./LLG 2, was the Ju 52 pilot for the first towed

A view of the DFS 230 V7, a larger version of the DFS 230. Note the loading door was in the roof of the fuselage, which probably accounts for the official lack of enthusiasm.

The DFS 331 first flew towards the end of 1940 but was not preferred to the Gotha Go 242.

flight and he recalled: "On 27 September 1940 I was ordered to fly Ju 52 'HS+BH' fitted with glider towing equipment to Gotha where flight testing of a new type was to take place under the authority of a Flugkapitän whose name I no longer recall. There were two airfields at Gotha, one used by the Luftwaffe and the other belonging to the Gothaer Waggonfabrik. It turned out that the Flugkapitän in question had not towed a glider before and when told of my experience (Ében-Émael, Drontheim/Norway) put a phone call through to the RLM to suggest that myself and my crew be retained for the flight trials.

"A telex order confirming this came through and my crew and I were sworn to secrecy and put up in a Gothaer hotel for the duration. On the following day we were taken to view the DFS 331 for the first time in its hangar where it was being prepared for flight testing. The type had been designed and built by a 20-strong team of DFS Flugingenieure under Hans Jacobs and was designed to carry up to 30 men. I was then introduced to Flugkapitän Hanna Reitsch who would be at the controls of the new glider.

"Both Reitsch and the test engineers again questioned me closely on my experiences as a glider tow pilot. My responses seem to satisfy them as did those of my unit. Fine weather the following day, 30 September, saw us make the first test runs with the glider in tow. However, the glider remained on the ground at that stage – Reitsch ordered us to release the tow-rope as we got airborne. We completed a circuit and after landing prepared for the first flight of the glider itself which took place late that afternoon and lasted 22 minutes. Everything ran without a hitch.

"The glider made over 100 test flights and had very pleasant handling qualities which were confirmed by Flugkapitän Francke from Rechlin. In the meantime, the Go 242 had made its first flight (9 November 1940) from the Gothaer Waggonfabrik works strip – I was at the controls of the Ju 52 tow plane and made two further flights on 9 and 10 November 1940. While development of the Go 242 proceeded – as far as I'm aware because loading and unloading operations proved easier – work on the DFS 331 was brought to an end on the orders of the RLM on 24 March 1941."

INDEX